Grandpa's Secrets

Unleash Your Awesomeness

By
Richard O'Keef
(Grandpa)

ISBN 978-0-9787884-6-9

Contents

My Promise to You.. 1

First, and Most Important: Who You Are.................... 2

The Church of Jesus Christ of Latter-Day-Saints 6

Baptism 7

The Holy Ghost.. 8

Jesus Christ 10

Suffering...11

You Might Be Someone's Answer to a Prayer........... 13

Life Hacks 14

A Person's Name is Dear to Them 14

Addiction.. 14

Money 16

Pin Your Socks Together 17

Sing and Dance 17

Be Generous 17

Clean Up as You Cook 18

Listen... 18

That's Gotta be Hard 19

Don't be Afraid to Say No 20

Focus on What You Can Control 20

The way Someone Treats You is a Reflection of How They Feel About Themselves 20

We Can't Change the Past 21

Never Give Up 21

Slurp Eggnog 22

Be Courageous 22

Be Authentic 22

Compliment Someone Everyday 22

Remember People's Birthdays 22

Family 23

Parenting 24

How to Enjoy Being a Parent 24

The 4 Emotional Needs 26

15 Parenting Skills 27

Skill #1: Spend One-On-One Time 28

Skill #2: Spend Family Time Together 30

Skill #3: Get to Know Your Children 32

Skill #4 – Make Positive Emotional Deposits 35

Skill #5: Give Choices 41

Skill #6: Teach Life-Skills 44

Skill #7: Help Children Set and Achieve Goals 50

Skill #8: Acknowledge Negative Feelings 54

Boundaries 65

Skill #9: Give Attention to Good Behavior 66

Skill #10: Getting Kids to Listen 70

Skill #11: Teach values 73

Skill #12: Create Rules 77

Skill #13: Enforce Rules 82

Skill #14: Use Consequences Wisely.......... 90

Skill #15: Problem-Solve Together............. 95

Common Situations and How to Approach Them 105

Tantrums... 105

Aggressive Behavior 108

Lying 111

Sibling Rivalry 115

Disrespectful Backtalk 121

Why I Wrote this Book 125

Dedication 127

Please Leave a Review............................. 129

My Promise to You

During your lifetime, you will see many things around you in a state of turmoil and chaos. I want you to not only survive in those conditions, but to thrive. I wrote this book so you will.

As I write this, the year is 2025 and I am 73 years old. I have 6 children, 23 grandchildren, and 5 great-grandchildren.

My life of experiences has taught me things that I do not want to take to my grave. I want to pass them on to you with a promise, that if you practice what I'm going to tell you, **you will be happier and feel more at peace**. Along with that promise, I also give you a warning: If you DO NOT practice what I'm about to tell you, you will struggle. As bold as that might sound, I'm confident it is true.

If you and I were having lunch together and you asked me, "What are some secrets you've learned during your life that you can pass on to me to make my life better?" I would tell you what you are about to read on the following pages. I would also feel honored that you would ask me. As it is, I feel honored that you are reading this book.

These secrets are the greatest gifts I can give you. They are a shortcut to unlocking your awesomeness and building a life that you can look back on with few regrets.

First, and Most Important: Who You Are

You are literally a child of God.

It is important to know who you are because Satan and the world will try to confuse you. They will try to convince you that you are just a child of this world and that it doesn't matter how you live or what you do. That's a lie.

Satan and the world would have you believe that it doesn't matter how you live your life. They would have you go after worldly pleasures and immediate gratification. They want you to forget you have a birthright to inherit all that the great king of the universe has waiting for you after this life.

You are not here (on this earth) now by chance. You have an important mission and purpose for being here on earth at this time. You have been saved to come into the world at this time to help usher in the second coming of Jesus Christ.

To make clear who you are and what your purpose is, let me suggest this metaphor.

Imagine you are on a team in the NBA finals (National Basketball Association championship) or the Superbowl (football). A win would make you the world champion. You are in the last few minutes of the game. The score of your team and the other team is very close. Who is your coach going to put into the game to increase your team's chance of winning? His best players, of course. He would put in the players in whom he had the most confidence; the players who have proven themselves in the past. He would be foolish not to do that.

Now consider this.

You have been sent to earth in the final part of the latter-days; the final minutes of the championship game when the battle between good and evil is the fiercest it's ever been; when the battle is the most heated it's ever been, because Satan knows he doesn't have much time left.

You have been sent **at** this time and **for** this time. What does that say about who you are? What does that say about who you were before you came to earth, and the confidence your Father in Heaven has in you to send you at this time? What does that say about your mission and purpose of being here.

Russel M. Nelson said, "Our Heavenly Father has reserved many of His most noble spirits—perhaps, I might say, His finest team—for this final phase. Those noble spirits—those finest players, those heroes—are you!" (Worldwide Youth Devotional • June 3, 2018 • Conference Center, Salt Lake City, Utah)

You are among Heavenly Father's most noble spirits in whom Heavenly father has the utmost confidence, **and it is my honor to be your grandpa.**

The world needs you. Go out there and influence the world for good as a disciple of Jesus Christ. Don't allow Satan and the voices of the world to influence you and convince you that you are merely a son or a daughter of "men". When you understand deep in your heart that you are a beloved son or daughter of God, you become empowered to overcome Satan and his influence.

By knowing who you are and who you were before coming to this earth, and by being valiant in keeping God's commandments, you will have lasting peace, joy and happiness not only here and now, but into the eternities.

Nothing the world can offer you compares to what your Heavenly Father desires to give you, and He can deliver on his promises the way the world never can.

But Satan will not stop trying to convince you otherwise. He is your enemy. Stay close to Heavenly Father and Jesus Christ so you won't be deceived. Satan has thousands of years of experience deceiving God's sons and daughters and he is very good at it. He will make a path look enticing, that will ultimately lead to regret and heartache. YOU ALONE ARE NO MATCH FOR HIM. Stay firmly connected to God to receive His divine power and protection through:

1. Daily prayer
2. Daily scripture reading
3. Daily repentance
4. Putting good things into your mind

5. Working to maintain a healthy body
6. Serving others

You will never regret doing these six things. They will bring you the most happiness and empower you to influence others. Others will look to you and think, "I'd like to be more like that person." I would not tell you unless I knew it.

How do I know it?

From time to time, I neglect to follow my own advice and disregard one or more of these six things. I put off prayer, scripture reading, repenting, my mental and physical health and/or serving others. When I do, I feel hollow, lost; like something is wrong. I feel heavy, anxious, and restless. That's a reminder for me to get back on the right path. When I do, I feel like things are right again. I feel peace of mind.

Practicing these six things will enable you to have an influence on others. Currently, I am a teacher. I teach fatherhood skills to incarcerated men in the state prison and county jail. When I am doing these six things, I develop a connection with my students in such a profound way, that they make comments like: "If I had a dad like you, I wouldn't be in jail", or, "Will you adopt me?"

If you are feeling like something isn't right, focus on putting these six things into practice.

The Church of Jesus Christ of Latter-Day-Saints

I want you to know that I know that this is the only church on earth that is directed by Jesus Christ, Himself, through a living prophet. It is Jesus Christ's church. This is the *only* church to have the authority to perform the ordinances necessary to bless you (and me) with eternal life.

What is eternal life? We don't know a lot about it, but what we do know can inspire us to want to receive it. Simply stated, eternal life is to live forever with our family in the presence of God. It means to inherit all that God has, and live in the highest state of happiness. It means to learn and progress until we become like God Himself. He **wants** us to become like Him.

How do I know?

I had an experience with the Holy Ghost.

There is a formula given to us by Heavenly Father to know that the Church of Jesus Christ of Latter-Day Saints is the only church on earth directed by Jesus Christ, Himself. You need only do three things to know this for yourself:

1) Read the Book of Mormon.

2) Ponder. Don't just try to get through the Book of Mormon as fast as you can. Take your time. Think deeply about what you're reading. Ask yourself,

was this book really written by ancient prophets for me to read today? And how can I apply what I am reading to my life?

3) Pray. Ask Heavenly Father whether or not the Book of Mormon is true. If you sincerely want to know, the Holy Ghost will bless you with an unmistakable feeling that the Book of Mormon is true and that the Church of Jesus Christ of Latter-Day Saints is the right church for you.

Baptism

When you are baptized into the Church of Jesus Christ of Latter-Day-Saints, you will be baptized by immersion. In other words, you will be put under the water and brought up out of the water by someone holding authority, symbolizing a rebirth—a new you. Shortly after that, someone with authority will lay his hands on your head and say these words: "I confirm you a member of the Church of Jesus Christ of Latter-Day-Saints and say unto you, **receive the Holy Ghost**."

When you are baptized, you covenant (or promise) to live God's commandments the best you can. And God makes a covenant with you. He promises that the Holy Ghost will always be with you to guide you, inspire you, and lift you. You'll feel the Holy Ghost in your life every day. But if you stop trying to live God's commandments, you will feel the influence of the Holy Ghost leave you. You'll feel empty and alone.

I know this to be true.

How do I know?

The Holy Ghost

I can feel when I have the Holy Ghost guiding me and when I don't.

The Holy Ghost helped me learn Japanese during my mission to Japan. More recently, the Holy Ghost guided me to get my current job as a Fatherhood Educator at the State Prison and county jails. Here's what happened.

In the spring of 2016, I was interested in helping parents become better parents. I had learned a few things about parenting over the years by reading dozens of parenting books. One day I had arrived to pick up mother (Nicolet, my wife) at Intermountain Medical Center after she got off work as a phlebotomist. I arrived early and decided to grab a bite to eat in the cafeteria. The cafeteria was nearly empty. On one of the tables lay a newspaper. I had never seen a newspaper in the cafeteria before, and I had eaten there many times. I picked it up to read while I ate my grilled cheese sandwich. When I came to the "help wanted" section, instead of skipping over it like I would normally do, I decided to read some help want-ads. This ad came to my attention:

NOW HIRING
Fatherhood Education Coordinators
Utah State University Extension
Logan, UT
Jobs.usu.edu

I was intrigued. I ripped out the ad, took it home and looked it up on the website listed. The job description sounded like something I would enjoy doing so I emailed a resume even though the cutoff date for applications had passed. They called me for an interview. Out of 209 people who applied for that position, I was one of 10 people they chose to teach parenting skills throughout Utah. I still have the ad.

I taught parenting classes at Wasatch Elementary School library, Jewish Community Center, at a Presbyterian Church, and other locations around Salt Lake City. I also taught incarcerated men at Salt Lake County Jail, Fortitude Treatment Center (a halfway house), and Utah State Prison. As I write this, I am currently teaching fatherhood education at Weber County Jail and Utah State Prison—nine years after I saw that ad.

Had I not arrived early, and had that newspaper not been there, and had I not seen it and picked it up, and had I not read the Help Wanted section and seen the ad, I wouldn't be teaching incarcerated men how to be good dads and helping them to change their lives. As it is, I've taught hundreds of students how to be good men and good dads.

Was there a divine hand in all this? Did the Holy Ghost guide me? I have no doubt.

By the way, I feel the Holy Ghost helping me write this book. Seriously, I'm not a very good writer by myself.

Jesus Christ

Here is what I want to tell you about Jesus Christ, and I can do it in just six paragraphs.

2000 years ago, when Jesus Christ walked on this earth as a mortal person, he organized a church called the Church of Jesus Christ. He taught that his church was the only true and living church upon the face of the whole earth. He taught that only His church held the laws, principles, doctrine, ordinances, authorities, and keys necessary to save and exalt men and women in the highest heaven hereafter.

He proclaimed that He, as the son of God, had come to work out the infinite and eternal atonement so that immortality would come to all as a free gift, while those who kept his laws and commandments would inherit eternal life.

He taught that eternal life comes by 1) faith (or belief) in Jesus Christ, 2), repentance, 3) being baptized in water by immersion by someone with the proper authority, 4) receiving the gift of the Holy Ghost by the laying on of hands, and 5) doing one's best to live the laws and commandments of Jesus Christ until death.

He taught that by doing these five things, men and women would have peace in this life and eternal life in the world to come.

That is exactly and identically what the Church of Jesus Christ of Latter-Day-Saints teaches, because it is Jesus Christ's restored Church.

As we focus our lives around Jesus Christ, we change what we desire. We change how we spend our time, what we read, what we watch, who we hang out with, and the choices we make. Our very nature is changed. Our spirit gains the power to have total control over our physical bodies. No longer will we seek after immediate pleasures and instant gratification in search of happiness, because we will have found it.

Suffering

Everyone goes through periods of suffering. It's part of life. People ask, "If God is a loving god, why does he allow people to suffer?"

People in my church tell me that God allows people to suffer and struggle so that they can become like Him. I have a hard time with that because I hate to see anyone suffer. Can't we be like him without suffering?

Here's what I have discovered. The times I have suffered has given me more ability to have patience and empathy with others who are suffering; who are lonely; who have had loss. It makes me more capable to reach out and serve in ways that I could not have done without suffering. As I think about this, I realize that having gone through difficult emotional states has given me the ability to help others with understanding and authenticity.

I went without a steady job for a year-and-a-half. I constantly worried about how I was going to support my family and pay the bills. This experience helped me relate with people in similar situations.

Suffering can either drive me away from God as I express my anger toward Him, or draw me closer to God as I seek for His help in getting through my suffering.

Since suffering is inevitable, I try to keep an eternal perspective, patiently trusting that my pains and sorrows will make me more like Heavenly Father and Jesus Christ, and eventually come to an end. It's just that it's hard to keep that in mind when I'm in the middle of a loss or a crisis.

I guess the bottom line is that everyone goes through trials. Everyone goes through suffering to one degree or another. It's part of life. But what matters is where we focus. Do we focus on the suffering and try to find someone or something to blame, or do we look ahead and try to make our lives better, not in spite of our suffering, but because of our suffering?

If we are going to praise the name of Heavenly Father and Jesus Christ in the good times, then we should continue to praise their names in the bad times.

I love what Linda S. Reeves said regarding trials in the General Woman's Session of October 2015 General Conference:

"Sisters, I do not know why we have the many trials that we have, but it is my personal feeling that the reward is so great, so eternal and everlasting, so joyful and beyond our understanding that in that day of reward, we may feel to say to our merciful, loving Father, 'Was that all that was required?' I believe that if we could daily remember and recognize the depth of that love our Heavenly Father and our Savior have for us, we would be willing to do anything to be back in Their presence again, surrounded by Their love eternally. What will it matter, dear sisters, what we suffered here if, in the end, those trials are the very things which qualify us for eternal life and exaltation in the kingdom of God with our Father and Savior?"

You Might Be Someone's Answer to a Prayer

Here is something that a very wise friend told me. He has been through a great deal of emotional pain during his life. He says *look at anybody. You don't know what trials they've been through or the hardships they are going through now. They may be overwhelmed with sadness, loneliness, or depression, but not show it outwardly.* So have compassion for everyone. You might be someone's answer to a prayer.

Life Hacks

I started this book by talking about spiritual secrets. I did that because those secrets will put you on a path to happiness more than anything else can. Now, I'm going to turn my attention to life hacks. There are tons of life hacks; things you can do to solve problems or make your life better. I've listed a few here.

A Person's Name is Dear to Them

You honor someone by learning their name, remembering it, and using it next time you see them. When you meet someone for the first time and find out their name, remember it. You can do this with word association or by writing it down. Then, next time you see them, call them by name. You will make them feel important. I have a terrible time remembering names, so I keep a skinny little note book in my shirt pocket. I will even say, "May I write your name down so I can remember?" I think that gives them a feeling that I care.

Addiction

One of the best ways to screw up your life is to become addicted to something.

I teach fatherhood education to incarcerated men in the Utah State Prison and in various county jails. I would guess that 90% of my students are drug addicts. Some of my students have been drug dealers. I've learned about addiction from them.

One of my students told me there are three reasons that children start using drugs:

1. Curiosity
2. To numb emotional pain
3. Peer pressure

Other reasons exist but they all relate to these three. Me and mother had a friend (we don't know where she is now) who was offered opioids and got addicted to them. She had a good job, a wonderful husband, two great children, and lost them all due to her addiction. She eventually turned to heroin and other drugs that controlled her life and ruined it.

You can become addicted to a drug after one try. So don't even try it once.

The chances are good that you will be offered drugs. Please be prepared to say no before that happens.

There are other addictions. They include:

- Social media
- Alcohol
- Smoking
- Pornography
- Junk food

I hope that you will avoid anything that promises a thrill or immediate pleasure, but ultimately results in unhappiness; anything that leads to addiction.

Money

Here are 5 things mother and I did that helped eliminate anxiety about money. 1) Make a monthly budget. We started on paper and then graduated to an Excel spreadsheet. List your monthly income and all expenses you expect for the month. If your expenses exceed your income, you have two options: Make more money, or eliminate some expenses. Then stick to your budget. 2) Use a debit card to pay for food and daily expenses. Every month, put money on your debit card according to your budget. When your debit card is near empty, you are done spending for the month. Mother and I had a $100 buffer that kept us from over-drafting. 3) Stay out of debt. If you use a credit card, pay it off every month. Because of high interest rates, making monthly payments on a credit card is throwing money away. 4) Put money away for a rainy day. For example, mother and I have an account with Fidelity that withdrawals a set amount of money from our bank account every month (budgeted in, of course). Then when it comes time to pay our annual homeowner's insurance and property tax, the money is there. We also contribute, monthly, to the following accounts at our bank or credit union for when needed: Emergency fund, medical expense, car insurance, vacations, and family reunions. 5) Pay tithing.

When you pay your tithing, you have Heavenly Father's promise that He will bless you. Mother and I have always had enough money, and we attribute that to paying tithing. I know you will be blessed when you have faith and pay your tithing.

Pin Your Socks Together

This saves time matching socks after washing.

Sing and Dance

Singing and dancing is good for you. It relieves stress and makes you feel good. Do it alone or with the people you love. Mother used to sing with our children at home and in the car. We danced with our children when they were little. Turn up the music and let yourself go.

Be Generous

If you want to feel good, be generous with your time and your money. Any time you help someone, you help yourself. You feel good.

Mother and I were having lunch at Chick-Fil-A with our daughter Sarah and her family. One of the little girls knocked over a large cup of soda and it went all over the floor. A young employee came over and cleaned up the mess. Mother and I gave him $20 for his effort. It made him light up and it made us feel good.

Be a big tipper at restaurants.

Go out of your way to help someone. Mother and I have a neighbor who is old. She calls us from time to time to help with various household tasks. It's usually inconvenient, but when we're finished, we feel good.

Serving others is a good way to change your mood from feeling depressed to feeling better.

I've never felt bad after being generous.

Clean Up as You Cook

You will eliminate a crazy amount of dishes to clean and won't have to leave a pile of dirty dishes overnight.

Listen

We all have two ears and one mouth to remind us that we should listen twice as much as we talk. Everyone has a basic human need to feel heard and understood. When that need is met, it makes people feel they are important and that they matter. When you listen without interrupting, you help meet that need. If you steer the conversation to be about yourself, you don't meet that need. If you want to make a difference in someone's life; if you want to strengthen your relationship with that person, listen twice as much as you talk.

Sometimes we highjack the conversation as soon as the other person takes a breath because what they are saying reminds us of an experience that we just can't wait to share. You can't listen when you're talking.

A good listener will listen to what the other person is saying without interrupting, nod occasionally, ask questions to make sure they understand, and then say what that person must be feeling: "That must be frustrating," or, "That's gotta make you feel good."

"Well, who is going to listen to me?" you might be asking. Don't worry. When the other person feels heard and understood, that person will listen to you.

It's easy for us to judge others. However, we don't know what they are going through or what led them to be the way they are. It's much easier to listen if we don't judge.

That's Gotta be Hard

Everyone has an emotional need to be heard and understood. Everyone—young and old. I'm going to teach you four words that will enable you to meet that need. First, listen to someone complain about their problem without interrupting. Then say, **"That's gotta be hard."** I teach this short phrase to my incarcerated dads who receive it with skepticism. But when they try using it, it changes their lives. Give it a try.

Don't be Afraid to Say No

That doesn't mean to defy your parents. It means to not take on more work or responsibility if it may threaten your mental well-being. Saying no is to set personal boundaries. It is a form of self-care and self-respect. Other's will respect you for it. When you say yes to everything, you risk burnout and resentment.

Focus on What You Can Control

You can't control what someone else does or says. You can only control your reaction. Your power lies in managing your own responses to the actions of others. When you control your reaction, you prevent anyone else from having a negative effect on you.

The way Someone Treats You is a Reflection of How They Feel About Themselves

That angry look? Not about you. That sarcastic comment? Not about you. Someone flips you off? Not about you. That temper tantrum? Not about you. The way a person behaves is all about their mental, physical, and spiritual state. They are having a bad day (or a bad life). Rather than taking offence, ask yourself, "What happened to you to make you do or say that?"

We Can't Change the Past

We can't change the past, so there's no point in living in it. Our past does not define who we are, although our past is a good teacher and we learn from it. The more we dwell on our past mistakes, the more depressed we become. So don't think about how your life could be different if only you had done things differently. Learn from it and move on.

But let's get real. It's hard not to have regrets. There was a time when I wanted to make some extra money for me and my family. I thought investing in the stock market would be the way to do that. I lost a lot of money. It still hurts to think about it. But there's nothing I can do to change that. So I have to leave it behind and move forward, and chalk it up to a life-lesson.

Never Give Up

This is a no-brainer. If you want to accomplish something, especially something difficult, you are going to encounter roadblocks (discouragement, people or circumstances that get in your way). If your "Why" is big enough, that is, if the reason for accomplishing that thing is important enough, you will never let discouragement, people, or circumstances keep you from achieving it.

You might lack skill, you might lack money, you might lack hope. But if you have grit, determination, and persistence, you will *always* accomplish the thing you are after. Never give up.

Slurp Eggnog

My children will tell you that I slurp eggnog and have invited them to do the same. I think it heightens the taste, and I like the sound.

Be Courageous

Courage is not the lack of fear. It is being afraid, and doing it anyway. Be courageous.

Be Authentic

Be willing to be vulnerable and face discomfort in order to express your true self (live in alignment with your values), even when it may not be popular or accepted. It takes courage to be authentic.

Compliment Someone Everyday

It will make you both feel good.

Remember People's Birthdays

It will make you both feel good.

Family

This is a tough one to write about because families can be different in so many ways. Having observed my children and their families, I came up with seven traits of a happy family. In a happy family, everyone:

1. Compliments each other
2. Helps each other
3. Encourages each other
4. Shows kindness
5. Celebrates one another's successes
6. Listens when someone is feeling down
7. Forgives

Ok, this may not happen often, but you can increase the chance it will happen more often by reading and practicing the remaining secrets. This entire book can be considered a blueprint to a happy family.

Families can be together even after we die. That's one of the reasons The Church of Jesus Christ of Latter-Day Saints builds temples. Please find out about temples and how they can bless your life.

The following secrets center around 5 powerful words. These 5 words have the potential to dramatically change your life by enabling you to make a positive impact on the people around you. They are the foundation, the key, to building strong relationships. Here are those words: *Meet the 4 Emotional Needs.* Are your four emotional needs being met?

Parenting

Even if you are not a parent, I want you to read my parenting secrets. They will teach you about the *4 Emotional Needs* that all human beings have. When you know about these 4 emotional needs, you will be empowered to create a deeper connection with anyone. You will understand what motivates people to behave the way they do, and how to have a greater influence.

If you are a parent, the following secrets will help you be a more competent, confident parent. I wish I had known these secrets when I was a young parent.

Over the years, I've read dozens of parenting books trying to figure out this crazy job of parenting. I think what I've learned and what I want to pass onto you will be enlightening.

How to Enjoy Being a Parent

When I was a young parent, I was clueless. I thought that when the time came for me to raise children, I would instinctively know what to do. That didn't happen. I was overwhelmed and stressed out. There came a point in time when I said to myself, "I had better make a serious change to the way I'm raising my children or me and my children will be in real trouble."

So I started reading parenting books.

The first thing I learned was how many parenting books there were. I asked myself, "If they all taught the same thing, then why so many?" And, "If they all taught something different, how many was I going to have to read to learn all the parenting skills I needed?"

As I went from one book to another, I made an interesting discovery. I discovered that all the good ones had one thing in common. They taught that children have emotional needs that must be met. I identified **four specific emotional needs** that I called: The 4 Emotional Needs. I learned that when parents meet these needs, good things happen:

1. Relationships with children grow stronger.
2. Cooperation improves.
3. Parents build strong families where children learn and practice good values.
4. Parents increase the odds that their children will make good choices even when parents are not around.

I also learned this.

If parents do NOT meet these four emotional needs, whether they know about them or not, that's when struggling happens. That's when children's behavior gets worse. That's when parents feel overwhelmed and stressed out. That's where I was. That was me: Overwhelmed and stressed out. So this was like a revelation to me.

The 4 Emotional Needs

Let me introduce you to the 4 Emotional Needs.

All children have a need for:

1. **A sense of belonging**. They want mom and dad's exclusive attention. They want to feel they are part of the family, feel important, significant, and that they matter.
2. **A sense of personal power**. They want to feel independent, autonomous, and do things their way. They don't like people telling them what they can and cannot do. They want to be able to make choices.
3. **To be heard and understood**. They want mom and dad to listen to them, and to acknowledge their feelings.
4. **Boundaries**. Boundaries make kids feel loved and cared for. But there are right and wrong ways to set and enforce boundaries.

After having discovered the 4 Emotional Needs, I went on to create a simple, easy-to-understand **formula** for raising children that's only five words long—but the most powerful five words a parent can live by:

Meet the 4 Emotional Needs.

When we meet the four emotional needs, good things happen. When we don't, everyone struggles.

15 Parenting Skills

There are 15 parenting skills that will empower parents to meet their children's four emotional needs. Here again are the needs and the skills to meet each need.

A sense of belonging:

> Skill #1: Spend One-On-One Time
> Skill #2: Spend Family Time Together
> Skill #3: Get to Know Your Children
> Skill #4: Make Positive Emotional Deposits

A sense of personal power:

> Skill #5: Give Choices
> Skill #6: Teach Life-Skills
> Skill #7: Help children set and achieve goals

To be heard and understood:

> Skill #8: Acknowledge Negative Feelings

Boundaries:

> Skill #9: Give Attention to Good Behavior
> Skill #10: Make Requests Effectively
> Skill #11: Teach values
> Skill #12: Create Rules
> Skill #13: Enforce Rules
> Skill #14: Use Consequences Wisely
> Skill #15: Problem-Solve Together

I've written a book about meeting the 4 Emotional Needs with the 15 Parenting Skills. The book is called: "*911,*

What is Your Parenting Emergency?" I want you to know about the 15 parenting skills now, so here is the condensed version of that book.

Skill #1: Spend One-On-One Time

This is the most important of all the parenting skills. If parents do not practice this skill, the rest of the skills will not work as well. If parents are struggling, Skill #1 is the place to start.

If you are having issues with your child such as

- whining
- clinging
- teasing
- not listening
- back-talking
- defiance
- or fighting with siblings,

spending one-on-one time with your child is the first thing you need to do, because **these are not discipline problems, these are relationship problems. And one-on-one time strengthens relationships.**

The skill works like this:

Each parent
Spends uninterrupted time
With each child
Every day (or as often as possible)

Doing what the child likes to do.

Simple as that.

Here are some things I used to do with my children.

1. Lie on the trampoline (or grass) at night with blankets and pillows and look at the stars
2. Play catch
3. Play a game—Old Maid is a card game with matching cards. Turn them all face down and take turns flipping over two cards, trying to find the matching pair
4. Shoot some hoops
5. Take a trip to the library
6. Bake something: cake, cookies, brownies
7. Build something with blocks or Legos
8. Draw or color something
9. Go to a golf course. Practice putting on the putting green, hit a bucket of balls, or play a round.
10. Build a snowman
11. Have a picnic—outdoors or indoors
12. Take the dog to a training class
13. Write a letter to someone you both know, like Grandma, or a friend
14. Build a blanket fort
15. Go to the park
16. Finger Paint with chocolate pudding
17. Fly a kite
18. Go on a bike ride

19. Read a book together
20. Lay in bed together at bed-time and just talk

Skill #2: Spend Family Time Together

Family activities promote family bonding and strengthen relationships between you and your children. They also strengthen relationships between siblings. They create good memories. Years later when your children are older, they will talk about the good times you spent doing things together. Remember to take pictures and record family events in a journal. Here are some things we used to do as a family:

1. Movie night with lots of popcorn
2. Bowling
3. Swimming and water amusement parks
4. Picnics
5. Hiking
6. Biking
7. Spending time at the park
8. Going out for ice cream
9. Flag football
10. Kickball
11. Kite flying
12. Miniature golf
13. Around the world Frisbee. Make a huge circle and toss two Frisbees around the circle at the same time.
14. Jump rope
15. Eat together as a family

Eat Dinner Together

Eating dinner together as a family provides opportunities for talking, catching up, and reconnecting. Studies have shown that when families regularly eat together, and the conversation is positive, children are more likely to exhibit good behavior.

Dinner time should not be a time to correct behavior, criticize, or blame. It should be an occasion when everyone feels safe and looks forward to being together—and oh yeah, no cell phones.

Involve Your Children in Your Life

Your children need to feel a sense of belonging; to feel needed, important, and that they matter.

So, involve them in your life by allowing them to help you.

When baking, let them help pour something into the bowl.

When washing the car, let them squirt off the soap with the hose.

You can say, "If I get you something to stand on, can you wash this plate?"

Before going into the grocery store, tell your child that you are on a mission and you need their help. Say, "We need milk, cheese, bread, and eggs. You remember the milk and cheese, and I'll remember the bread and eggs. I think if you help me, we can remember everything."

Skill #3: Get to Know Your Children

Each one of your children has likes, dislikes, opinions, worries, fears, wishes and beliefs, whether you know about them or not. If your children feel safe talking about these things, your connection with them will grow stronger and they will become more open to your influence.

Sometimes children **want** to talk, but they are not ready to talk. Their body language will tell you that something is wrong. So you can say,

> *You seem a little down today...*
> *You seem a little distracted today...*
> *You seem angry...*

Use "You seem ____" to make an observation, and then follow up with,

> *Is there anything you want to talk about?*

If they decline, follow up with,

> *Okay. When you're ready, I'm here.*

When your child is ready to open up, try not to look panic-stricken if they drop a bomb on you. "Dad, I'm pregnant." Mom "I have a drug habit that I need help with." It's important to stay calm.

Ultimately, you want your kids to feel safe talking with you, which means, they will not worry about you laughing, criticizing, judging or getting upset. You want them to walk away feeling like you have their back. When that happens, they will be more likely to have similar conversations again.

Provide an environment conducive to talking. That would include: while eating a meal together, while preparing a meal together, during one-on-one time, or while driving in the car (turn off the radio). In all these cases you are not making constant eye contact and that can make it easier for your children to open up.

Ask Questions That Cause Them to Think

Here are some possible questions to get the ball rolling:

Toddlers and Little kids

- What is your favorite animal?
- What is your favorite color?
- What is your favorite dessert?
- What is your favorite part of school?
- What makes you happy?

Age 5-12

- What is something you do not like?
- What is something you are afraid of?
- What food do you love, and what food do you hate?
- If you could be any animal, what would you be?

- What if you were alone with a teacher, family member or neighbor, and they touch you in places that make you feel uncomfortable, or ask you to touch them? What should you say and what should you do?
- If you could have a super power, what would it be?
- If someone offered you drugs, what would you do? What should you do?

Age 13-18

- If you could have any wish, what would it be?
- If you won a million dollars, what would you do?
- What is your dream job?
- What skill would you like to learn?
- When you do something hard, what keeps you from quitting?
- You are on a date with someone you really like, and they begin to pressure you to have sex. What do you say and do?
- If someone tried to pick a fight with you, what would you do? If someone tried to pick a fight with your friend, what would you do?

Author Catherine M. Wallace has written something that I'd like to pass on to you:

Listen earnestly to anything your children want to tell you, no matter what. If you don't listen eagerly to the little stuff when they are little, they won't tell you the big stuff when they are big. Because to them, all of it has always been big stuff.

For more possible questions to ask, go to Google and search on:

> Questions to ask 5-year-olds
> Questions to ask 10-year-olds
> Questions to ask ___ year-olds
> Questions to ask teenagers

Skill #4 – Make Positive Emotional Deposits

If you have a high, positive balance in your child's emotional bank account, the level of trust is high, communication is open and free, and your ability to influence that child is increased dramatically.

In his book, *The 7 Habits of Highly Effective Families*, Stephen R. Covey teaches how to improve relationships with your children by using the analogy of an emotional bank account.

You make deposits by doing things that build trust. You make withdrawals by doing things that decrease trust. Examples of making withdrawals would be nagging, criticizing, and losing your temper.

If you have a low balance or are overdrawn, there is little or no trust, no real communication, and your ability to influence that child is decreased considerably. Here are

10 deposits you should make to ensure a high, positive balance.

1. Be Thoughtful

Say please, thank you, and excuse me. Do small favors. Call just to say "Hi." Express appreciation. Give sincere compliments. Tuck a note in a lunchbox. Write an inspiring note and stick it on the mirror or somewhere they will see it. Fix a favorite breakfast. Attend games, plays and recitals in which your child is participating. Look for opportunities to be thoughtful. When you do, you'll find them everywhere.

2. Make Hello and Goodbye a Special Event

In the morning when you first see your children, greet each one like they were an important person: "Good morning. How did you sleep?" Be sure to say goodbye with a hug or a fist-bump to each child before you leave for work.

When you get home from work, seek out each child to say hello. Don't forget to make children feel important when they go to bed at night by saying good night and giving a hug and an, "I love you." This gives them a boost of positive attention and meets their need for a sense of belonging.

3. Apologize when Necessary

Some parents think that apologizing is a sign of weakness, when in fact, just the opposite is true. Apologizing turns withdrawals into deposits. "I said some things that were unkind and I want to apologize. I was angry, but I should not have said what I did." We all make mistakes. When we do, we need to own up to it, sincerely apologize, and move on. The outcome will be far better than trying to hold on to stubborn pride.

4. Keep Promises

Promises create excitement, anticipation and trust. Broken promises create disappointment and mistrust. Make your word your bond. If you tell your child to expect something, do everything in your power to see it through.

This goes for discipline as well. If you tell your child at the store, "If you take one more thing off the shelf, I'll take you home and come back by myself," you need to follow through. Otherwise, you child will not take you seriously when set rules and expectations.

5. Forgive

Your children will give you many opportunities to practice forgiveness. Forgiveness will free you from the burden that anger places on you. It releases the bitterness and resentment you feel when your children are inconsiderate, uncooperative, rude, disrespectful or rebellious. Don't stop forgiving. Don't hold a grudge. You don't have to say, "I forgive you" out loud, just say it in your heart and mind.

6. Laugh Together

Besides strengthening your immune system, boosting your energy, and reducing stress, laughing together with your kids is a good bonding activity. Kids like being with you when you make them feel good, and laughing makes them (and you) feel good. Laughing with your children:

- Strengthens your relationship
- Allows your children to express their deeply felt emotions more freely
- Gives your children a good dose of acceptance and a sense of belonging

Ask your kids if anything funny happened to them today.

Laughter must be shared by everyone. If someone is the brunt of a joke or the object of sarcasm, then your laughter takes on the form of criticism and shame, and harms your relationship—even if you say, "Just kidding."

7. Touch in Gentles Ways

Appropriate touching can be a powerful way to increase bonding, cooperation, and teamwork within our families. Babies actually need loving touch to develop properly, both physically and emotionally. As children grow, it can be hard to maintain a culture of touching, so here are some suggestions to get you in the habit.

Give hugs every day when kids are small, make it a routine to hug your children when they get up, when they're leaving for school, when they get home, and before bed.

Even teens need hugs – maybe not as often as small children, but they need them. My kids are in their 30's and 40's and we still hug. I hug all 23 of my grandchildren interspersed with fist-bumps.

8. Read Together

Studies have shown that reading to children helps them develop language skills, problem-solving skills, creativity and empathy. When they go to school, they tend to do better. Reading to children will bring the two of you closer together.

9. Say I Love You

Some parents have a hard time saying, "I love you" to their children. Maybe it was never said to them. Here are some things that happen to children when they hear "I love you." It makes them feel important. It gives them the freedom to make mistakes. It gives them confidence. It gives them courage. It helps them to love others. It creates a desire to love you back. Try a little experiment. Next time, instead of saying, "I love you," say, "I love being your dad." "I love being you mom." You will get an out-of-the-ordinary reaction.

10. Dad, Mom, Treat Each Other with Kindness and Respect

Children notice how you treat each other, whether you live together or not. Dad, your actions teach your sons how to treat a woman and teach your daughters what to look for in a future husband. If either of you use belittling comments, verbal abuse, yelling, criticism, sarcastic remarks, verbal threats, unwanted physical contact, rudeness, or show disrespect whether to each other or behind each other's back, it will have a negative emotional effect on your entire family.

Because you set an example of how to treat each other, you should also forbid your children from disrespecting mom or dad. Kids should know they are also expected to show kindness and respect. If your kids show disrespect, let them know you disapprove and correct their behavior by using the skills taught in this book.

And dad, when the end of your workday rolls around, take the kids off mom's hands. Do not be the kind of man who thinks housework and raising children are for women only. Give her all the help you can. Make positive deposits into *her* emotional bank account.

Skill #5: Give Choices

Giving children choices gives them a **sense of personal power**, and when a child has a couple of options to consider, putting up a struggle might not even cross her mind.

All kids have a need for a sense of personal power. Personal power means to feel in control of one's self or the situation. It means having the freedom to choose. Kids want to feel empowered and significant. They don't like feeling controlled by someone else.

Children who do not have a strong relationship with parents, do not like their parents telling them what to do, so they rebel. They feel they can take back their personal power by 1) saying "no" to requests, 2) disregarding rules, and 3) doing the opposite of what parents ask. This usually results in a power struggle:

> "You'll do it because I said so."
> "No I won't."
> "Yes you will."
> "You can't make me."

When parents get into a power struggle, they never win.

However, giving children choices gives them a sense of personal power and reduces power struggles.

Give your kids a choice whenever you would normally choose something for them. Instead of giving them a breakfast cereal, offer them a choice: "Would you like this cereal or this cereal?" Or ask for their opinion: "Which soap should I put by the sink, the bar soap or the squirt soap?"

Offer two options, each of which you are OK with.

Here are some more examples:

- Do you want potato chips or corn chips in your lunch?
- Do you want the green towel or the blue towel?
- Do you want juice or milk?
- Which outfit do you want to wear, this one or this one?
- Shall we read this book or this book?
- Do you want to brush your teeth first or shall I brush your teeth first?

Offering choices is a simple but powerful way to give kids daily doses of personal power. You can also use choices to get kids to do something they don't want to do:

- Do you want to load the dishwasher or clean up dog poop?
- Would you like to clean the living room or the bathroom?
- Do you want to do your homework at the table or up to the counter?
- Do you want to brush your teeth in the bathroom or the kitchen?

- Would you like to go home now or in 10 minutes?

This is a simple skill but very powerful.

I was teaching a pre-school teacher who had a student that didn't like to take orders. She said it was time for the children to stop playing on the rug and sit up to the table. Her stubborn student ignored her request. Then she remembered what we talked about in class. She called him by name and said, "Do you want to sit in the red chair or the blue chair?" "Red chair," he said, got up, came over to the table and sat in the red chair.

One more.

My daughter and her family were visiting me and my wife. They had to leave in five minutes. My son-in-law made an announcement: "We need to go. Do you want to leave now or in five minutes?" "Five minutes," was the consensus. "Ok, I'm setting my alarm," he said. When the alarm went off, everyone got up and headed for the car without a bit of complaining.

If your child cannot make up her mind, you can say, "If you don't choose, then I will choose for you." If your child chooses something that was not one of the choices, you can make the choice for her.

- Dad: "Do you want milk or water?"
- Child: "Soda pop."
- Dad: "That wasn't one of your choices. Shall I choose for you?"

When do you use choices? Regularly throughout the day, whenever you would normally choose something for your kids. Instead of choosing for them, let them choose.

Skill #6: Teach Life-Skills

As a parent, what is it that you want to ultimately accomplish? My guess is that you want to see to it that your children learn to become independent adults, with the knowledge and ability to take good care of themselves and make good choices.

As important as that goal seems to be, it is my observation that many young adults are incapable of taking care of themselves because they have not been trained.

I see two reasons for this.

1. Parents feel that the way to communicate love for their children is by doing everything for their children; things that their children could be doing on their own.

2. Parents get worn out by the whining and complaining and feel it is just easier to do things for their children rather than make them do it themselves. In both cases, the parents are focusing on the moment, and not on the big picture.

Parents who keep their children's future in mind train their children in age-related skills and watch their children as they learn, struggle, make mistakes, figure it out and eventually thrive as they master those skills.

They watch their children's self-esteem grow as they take on the belief that *I can do this myself.*

They watch their children's self-confidence grow as their children take steps to become capable and independent.

Children lack vision.

That's why they have you. Your role as a parent is to take charge and be a leader. Your role is to train your children to be independent adults someday and give you grandchildren.

Then you can spoil all you want. But until then, you need to give your children the knowledge and ability to succeed in a tough world.

As a take-charge mom or dad (and the boss of your kids), you are going to experience frustration as your children resist and complain, "But why do I have to?"

You will look them in the eye and say, *"Because I have more information and experience than you do and I know what you're going to be up against when you strike out on your own. So, you can take comfort in knowing that I will do everything I can to get you prepared."*

Your children don't know it, but you are going to give them a gift that will benefit them for the rest of their lives: **the gift of knowledge and ability, and the gift of independence.**

Life-skills are skills that help children make the transition from dependence to independence by adding to their capabilities and helping them experience the joy that comes from achieving something through hard work, perseverance and patience.

When you teach children life-skills you empower them. You give them the ability, the confidence, and the *power* to do something they couldn't do before.

Life-skills include household responsibilities, but go beyond that.

They include anything that enriches someone's life, such as learning to count, throwing a ball, riding a bike, making a healthy smoothie, learning to swim, or riding a horse. As children are exposed to life-skills, they will decide what interests them and what doesn't.

Keep in mind that what interests you may not necessarily interest them. And what interests one child might not interest another. Exposing them to many life-skills will give them opportunities to *choose* what they like and what they don't like, and being able to *choose* helps satisfy their need for a sense of personal power.

Children are hard-wired with a need for a sense of belonging and personal power. Teaching them life-skills is a good way to satisfy both needs. You can give them a sense of belonging by spending time teaching them. You can give them a sense of personal power by empowering them with new skills.

I believe every child is born with unique talents and gifts. The more you expose your children to new life-skills, the greater the chance those unique gifts will be discovered. For example, a child may be born with the gift of singing. But unless that child is exposed to opportunities to sing, that gift may never be realized.

Here is a short list of life-skills I found on a website called "Indy's Child", written by Nicole Sipe. (https://indyschild.com/essential-life-skills-to-teach-kids-at-every-age)

Toddlers & Preschoolers

- Recite their first, middle and last name
- Put their dirty clothes in the hamper
- Feed and water the family pet with supervision
- Pull up and down their own pants
- Potty on the toilet
- Put on their shoes or boots
- Put on and take off their jacket
- Zip or button their clothes with some help
- Fold a blanket
- Throw away their trash after a snack
- Help clean up their toys
- Wash their hands properly for 20 seconds
- Brush and floss their teeth with lots of help and supervision
- Sort the dirty laundry by colors
- Put away clean utensils in their proper places

- Butter bread
- Help with preparing a meal
- Wipe up spills with a cloth

Early Elementary

- Learn their address
- Memorize mom and dad's phone number
- Learn how to make an emergency phone call
- Take out the trash
- Water the plants
- Put the wet, clean clothes in the dryer
- Brush their hair
- Pick out a coordinating outfit
- Change a toilet paper or paper towel roll
- Insert batteries into, or charge a flashlight
- Open the house door with a key
- Wash vegetables and fruit
- Set the table
- Pour their own glass of milk or juice into a cup
- Help make a grocery list
- Tie their shoes
- Get the mail
- Ride a bike without training wheels

Late Elementary

- Write thank-you notes
- Brush and floss their teeth on their own
- Make a sandwich or a simple snack

- Make their bed
- Fold towels and put them away
- Vacuum the rug
- Wrap a present
- Wash the dishes by hand
- Load and unload the dishwasher
- Use the microwave

Tweens

- Address, stamp and mail a letter
- Use a broom and dustpan properly
- Haul the trash bins to the curb
- Hammer a nail and hang a picture frame
- Fold or hang clothes
- Rake leaves and put them in bags
- Pull weeds
- Read nutrition labels and make good food choices
- Know the purpose of the appliances and tools in the kitchen and how to use them
- Feed and water the family pet independently
- Change their sheets and bedding
- Operate the washing machine and dryer, and know how much detergent to use
- Fold clothes and put them away

Teens

- Sort, wash, dry, fold/hang and put away laundry
- Iron a wrinkled shirt

- Prepare a simple dinner
- Clean the kitchen after making dinner
- Plunge a clogged toilet
- Diagnose simple illnesses, take their own temperature and learn proper medicine doses
- Make a budget and save money
- Learn what credit is and how to use it wisely
- Mow the lawn
- Do simple car maintenance tasks, like check the oil
- Change a tire
- Work a fire extinguisher
- Pump gas
- Memorize their social security number
- Pack a suitcase and determine what kind and how many clothes they might need for a trip
- Change a light bulb
- Locate and use the water shutoff valve
- Unclog a drain
- Reset a tripped fuse

Skill #7: Help Children Set and Achieve Goals

Achieving goals helps children feel a higher sense of self-worth, self-confidence, and a sense of personal power, all essential in overcoming challenges, becoming independent, and enjoying success. The following illustration shows, at a glance, how you can help your child set and achieve goals.

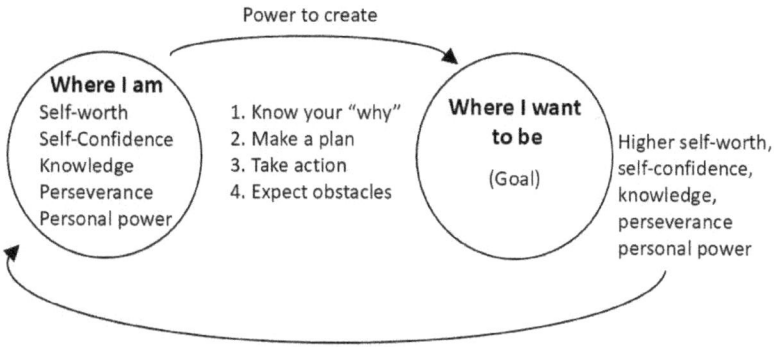

Power to create. Goals help a child learn something or do something or create something that was once non-existent. Teach your child that he or she has the power to create.

Where I am. This is your child's current self-worth, self-confidence, knowledge, strength of perseverance, and sense of personal power. When your child achieves his goal, all of these characteristics increase and make it possible to shoot for a bigger goal next time.

Where I want to be (the goal). What does your child want to achieve? What gets him excited? What does he or she dream about doing or having? Encourage your child to choose goals that are attainable but also just out of reach. That way he learns to push himself to meet a new challenge instead of remaining in the *comfort zone*.

Know your "why". This is the first step in the process to achieving a goal. If your child doesn't have a good reason to achieve his goal, he'll quit as soon as things get hard. When your child gets stuck, his vision, or reason for achieving his goal, will help him keep going.

Make a plan. Every goal that you can think of has already been achieved by someone who has given us a plan to follow. Look into books, videos, coaches, classes and mentors for that. Search the internet for any topic. Search YouTube for instructions on how to do almost anything.

Depending on the size of your child's goal, you might break his big goal into smaller, manageable steps. Make a *goal ladder* with his big goal at the top. Each rung on the ladder is a smaller step required to get to the top. Each step leads to the next. And when your child plans smaller steps along the way, it's easier to measure his progress.

Setting *realistic deadlines* makes it much more likely that you and your child will actually plan out each step to achieve your goals in a reasonable amount of time.

Take action. Now he or she must take "massive" action by following the plan.

Expect obstacles. Every goal worth achieving has obstacles along the way. When your child is faced with a task that seems too hard, talk about perseverance. Having perseverance means that you keep working on something that's hard or takes a long time to complete. When a child struggles to achieve a goal, the accomplishment of that goal is even sweeter. Help your child understand that challenges are opportunities to learn, and that overcoming challenges make us stronger and more resilient; able to tackle bigger challenges down the road.

When roadblocks come along, revisit the first three steps to achieving a goal. Is the "Why" still big enough? Do you need to revise your plan? Then take action.

Remember, you are your child's biggest cheerleader. Recognize and congratulate achievements made along the way. *Your recognition and congratulations will encourage him to keep going.*

When the Goal is Achieved

Look what happens when the goal or a step to the goal is achieved. Your child's sense of self-worth and self-confidence goes up. Knowledge and perseverance are increased. What he couldn't do before, he has learned to do, which gives him a healthy dose of personal power. All of these are added to "Where I am". And your child is empowered to take on a more challenging goal.

If the Goal is Not Achieved

What if your child gives up? What if the goal is out of reach or your child loses interest in pursuing the goal? How do you keep your child's self-worth, self-confidence, and sense of personal power from crashing down? That's where **unconditional love** comes into play.

Let your child know that even if he never achieves the goal, you still love him and you will never stop loving him. There will be other goals that you'll help him achieve as soon as he is ready. Then take him out for ice cream. Do something to meet his sense of belonging because right now he is feeling like he let you down.

Do not criticize. Criticism kills relationships.

Skill #8: Acknowledge Negative Feelings

The Danger of NOT Acknowledging Negative Feelings

One of the **biggest mistakes** parents make is to deny their children the opportunity to express negative feelings.

When children have negative feelings and no one will **listen** to them, they stuff those feelings down into their subconscious and that's where those feelings stay and accumulate.

Each time their feelings are **ignored** or **criticized**, it's like adding a brick to an imaginary backpack. Over time, that backpack gets very heavy and it takes energy to haul it around everywhere. That heavy backpack full of emotional bricks affects choices, relationships, and behavior.

I teach in the jail and the prison. I hear stories from my students about their upbringing, and my heart breaks when I hear how their feelings were discounted as unimportant when they were growing up.

It makes me wonder if their lives would have turned out differently if they had felt *heard and understood.*

We'll never know, but it's my opinion there are a lot of people who do drugs, drink, get involved with pornography, make babies, join gangs, and do crimes because they had no one who would listen to them when they were in distress.

11-year-old Johnny comes home from school and announces to dad, "My teacher's mean. She made fun of me in front of the whole class and everybody laughed. I hate her." Dad says, "Well maybe you should have followed instructions and that wouldn't have happened."

Dad did not meet Johnny's need to be heard and understood.

Johnny finds mom. "My teacher's mean. She made fun of me in front of the whole class and everybody laughed. I hate her," to which mom says, "Oh, honey, she probably didn't even know she hurt your feelings."

Mom did not meet Johnny's need to feel heard and understood.

Johnny confides in big brother. "My teacher's mean. She made fun of me in front of the whole class and everybody laughed. I hate her." "Dude," says big brother, "You've got to be tough. You can't let something like that bother you. Get over it and move on. Don't be a mama's boy. Be a man."

Big brother did not meet Johnny's need to feel heard and understood.

These are all examples of Johnny's feelings being denied. He can't get anyone to meet his need to feel heard and understood. He tries to push the emotional pain away but it never really leaves him.

The next day Johnny is at school walking down the hall and hears someone call out his name. "Hey, Johnny." It's an older boy who he's seen around but doesn't know. "Hey, I heard you took some heat from that teacher. That's f**ked up. Sorry to hear that, man."

"Oh, I'm ok." says Johnny.

The boy says, "Me and some guys, we hang out together and we're there for each other. You should come hang with us. We know how to make bad feelings go away."

What is the older boy trying to get Johnny to do? Join a gang? Try a drug? Do a crime? Just hang out? The point is, if Johnny's need to feel heard and understood is not met by his parents, he is going to be vulnerable to other people meeting that need; people who may not have his best interest at heart.

You argue, "That's not going to happen after one such incident."

That may be true, but if this need to be heard and understood continues to go unmet for a long time, the stored-up pain can result in Johnny's desire to numb his pain anyway he can.

That could include joining a gang, trying a drug, experimenting with alcohol, looking at porn, or having casual sex. His interest in school may drop. His desire to be a "good kid" may disappear. He may try to get back at his parents by doing things he knows they disapprove of. He may seek revenge.

When parents do not meet their child's need to be heard and understood, they put their children at risk. They distance themselves from their children and weaken their relationship. Their influence ceases.

Let's give our story a better ending. Johnny comes home from school and announces to dad, "My teacher's mean. She made fun of me in front of the whole class and everybody laughed. I hate her." Dad says, "In front of the whole class? That must have been embarrassing. Tell me more."

Here's How the Skill Works

When your child comes to you in distress, with a problem or hurt feelings, you **listen** without interrupting—even if you know what she is saying is not exactly the truth.

When your child is done venting, then you reflect what you heard. That means you say back to your child how she is feeling and why.

This will enable your child to calm down and let go of her negative feelings. If she is faced with a problem, acknowledging her feelings will put her in a state of mind to come up with ideas to solve that problem.

When you acknowledge negative feelings on a regular basis with all your children, they will feel more like approaching you when they have problems, even during their teenage years.

Acknowledging negative feelings provides emotional healing.

When a child comes to you in distress, she doesn't want you to agree or disagree; she doesn't need your opinion or advice. She doesn't want you to "fix it". What she wants and needs is for you to listen and show that you understand.

When you acknowledge negative feelings you:

1. Let the child say whatever she wants
2. Give her the freedom to express all kinds of nasty, critical things, whether they are true or not.
3. Allow her to vent.

And while this is happening, you listen. Then you reflect back to her, the emotion she must be feeling and the reason. *"She scribbled on your drawing after all that work you put into it. I can see why you are so mad."*

How to Acknowledge Negative Feelings

The hardest part about acknowledging negative feelings is taking the time to do it. When your child comes to you in distress, it's rarely at a convenient time. So you have to decide, "Do I take the time now, or do I postpone?" If you postpone, arrange a time to talk later.

There are three parts to acknowledging negative feelings:

1. Clarify
2. Listen
3. Reflect how the child is feeling and why

Step 1. Clarify

To clarify means to ask questions in order to understand the reason behind the distress. For example, your son doesn't want to go to school. You can clarify by using any of the following phrases:

- "Why don't you want to go to school?"
- "Why? What's going on?"

You can clarify by turning her statement into a question: "You don't want to go to school?"

You can clarify by encouraging her to continue: "Go on." Or "Tell me more."

When he is done explaining, you can clarify further by asking, "Hmm. I see. Is there anything else you want to tell me?"

Step 2. Listen

Give your full, undivided attention. No multi-tasking. If your phone rings, ignore it or tell the caller that you'll call them back. Just listen and nod occasionally. By giving undivided attention, you let the child feel important and loved; something that meets her need for a sense of belonging. Allow the child to say things even if you know they are not true. This is listening time, not correcting time.

Listening will often enable your child to let go of his negative feelings and fix the problem on his own. You'll know that your conversation is done when he says, "Thanks dad, see ya."

Step 3. Reflect How the Child is Feeling and Why

This is where you give a summary of **how the child is feeling** and **why he is feeling that way**. Some people call it *reflecting* because you reflect back to the child what you are understanding. Showing that you understand has two parts that you can use in any order:

1. Identify how the child is **feeling**
2. Summarize **why** the child is feeling that way

Feeling words

Use words that describe how the child is feeling. I call these "feeling words":

- Mad: "You are mad."
- Frustrating: "That can be so frustrating."
- Sucks: "Oh, man, that sucks."
- Disappointing: "How disappointing."
- Embarrassing: "That must have been embarrassing."
- "Ohh noo": This is a generic response to any distressful situation the child throws at you.
- "That's gotta be hard": another generic response to any distressful situation.

Reflect and Identify the Feeling

Here are some examples of ways to say how the child is feeling AND why the child is feeling that way.

Child: "I'd like to punch that Michael in the nose. We were playing soccer and he pushed me down."

You: "You were both going after the ball and he pushed you down, and that made you mad".

Child: "My teacher is stupid. Just because of a little rain she said we couldn't go on our field trip."

You: "You've been looking forward to going—how disappointing."

Child: "Basketball sucks. Tom and Bill made the team but I didn't."

You: "You were cut from the team? Ohh noo."

I use the following phrase all the time, and I advise my students to use it:

"That's gotta be hard," a short way to make people feel heard and understood.

The Spinning Chair

One day my grandchildren were visiting. four-year-old Brooklyn and her three-year-old brother, Stockton, came into the family room and spotted the spinning chair. The spinning chair is an office chair that the grandchildren love to sit on and spin around.

Both made a dash for the chair. Stockton got there first and climbed up onto it. I could see Brooklyn fuming and I was afraid she was going to do something mean to Stockton.

The first thing that came to my mind was to say, "Brooklyn. Let Stockton have a turn and then it will be your turn." That makes perfect sense, right? It's so logical. But kids don't think logically when they are in distress. They think emotionally.

I went over to Brooklyn, got on one knee so I was eye-to-eye with her and said, "Brooklyn. You are really mad. You wanted to beat Stockton to the chair and I think you even wanted him to push you around."

She didn't say a word, but I could see her whole body relax. She turned around and off she went.

You'll notice I didn't give advice, tell her to get over it, or tell her to stop being a baby. All I did was summarize **how** she was feeling and **why** she was feeling that way.

An Argument for Listening

I was teaching inmates at the county jail about fatherhood.

We were discussing values and consequences. One of my students stood up and said, "That's it. I'm out of here," and left the classroom.

I was afraid I had offended him in some way.

As we were wrapping up class, he walked back in and sat down. When class was over, everyone filed out except for him. I asked him what happened back there.

He said he disagreed with everything I said.

I'm OK with that. In fact, I welcome differences of opinion. I asked him to explain.

He said, "My parents raised me in a strict religious home. They tried to force their own values down my throat. When I didn't respond to their liking, they made up consequences and punishments to get me to conform."

He told me his parents read all kinds of self-help books to help them deal with him. He said they did the best they knew how, nevertheless, he rebelled.

Then he said something that I will never forget. He said, **"If my parents would have just sat down and had a decent conversation with me."**

What he said showed me that a child's feelings and opinions are important no matter how different they are from his parent's. And when a child wants to express those feelings, the parents would do well to acknowledge those feelings by listening and reflecting.

Had his parents taken time, regularly, to make their son feel heard and understood, would his life have turned out differently? Would he be in jail? No one can say, but I feel compelled to make this argument:

If you do not listen to your child; if you do not meet his or her need to feel heard and understood, your influence will dwindle. You will run the risk of experiencing a disconnection with your child and watch as your child spirals down into rebellion and unhappiness.

Criticism Kills Relationships

When you give unsolicited advice to teens and adults, it is often received as criticism, and criticism kills relationships. In the following conversation, what this child wants is a symptom of a deeper emotional issue.

Child: "I want to have blue hair"

Don't criticize. Repeat back and listen to the feeling behind the words.

You: (Clarify) "Oh, you wanna have blue hair?"

Then just be quiet.

Child: "Everyone's doing it."

You: "Sounds like you wanna be like the other kids."

Child: "Sometimes I feel like I don't fit in."

...Which is really the conversation you want to have.

When you acknowledge negative feelings, your children will be more willing to open up with you.

Boundaries

Skills 9 through 15 center around boundaries, the fourth of the 4 Emotional Needs.

"Boundaries" is composed of two parts: Teaching and Correcting. Teaching means teaching your children about your expectations, values and rules. Correcting is what you do when your children don't meet your expectations, ignore your values, or break your rules.

Here's the thing. If you do not have a strong relationship with you children, they won't care about what you teach them. And trying to correct their behavior will seem futile—because THEY WON'T CARE.

However, if you have a strong relationship, your children will be receptive to what you teach, and responsive when you correct their behavior. The way you strengthen your relationship is by meeting your children's first three emotional needs. Consider the following illustration.

The 4 Emotional Needs

1. A sense of belonging
2. A sense of personal power   } *Relationship*
3. To be heard and understood
4. Boundaries
   Teaching
   Correcting

When you develop a strong relationship FIRST, your teaching and correcting will be much easier. Connect before you correct.

Skill #9: Give Attention to Good Behavior

More than anything else, children want the attention of their parents. If they can't get it behaving *good*, they discover they can get it behaving *bad*. Kids learn that angry attention is better than no attention at all.

Please read the following statement carefully because it is the foundation of this skill and the reason it works.

The behavior that receives the most attention is the behavior that will happen the most.

Will you agree that most of the time, the behavior that receives the most attention is the bad behavior? Well, if the above statement is true, and I'm claiming it is, then the following statement must also be true.

If you pay more attention to good behavior, good behavior will happen more often.

Experts in child behavior say this is one of the best ways to replace misbehavior with cooperation. I've seen it work and I know parents who were amazed at how quickly their children's behavior changed when they applied this principle. Here is what you do:

Look for good behavior and give it attention.

Giving attention to good behavior means watching each of the children, and when one of them behaves in a good way, rewarding him or her with positive attention. Here are some examples:

- I noticed you were nice to your sister all morning.
- I noticed you came when I called the 1st time.
- I noticed you did the dishes without being asked.
- Thank you for cleaning up your spill.

Here is the challenge. Usually when children are behaving well, it's easy to ignore them. "Don't disturb them when they're happy," you might say.

Don't ignore children's good behavior. Watch for opportunities to give attention to good behavior.

Even children who are *always* misbehaving will accidently do something right. You might say, "I noticed you walked past your brother without teasing him. Thank you."

The more positive attention you give a child who exhibits good behavior, the more you will reinforce that behavior. You have to watch for opportunities. Sometimes you have to watch really hard.

Dr. Glenn I. Latham, in his book, *The Power of Positive Parenting*, states: "Research has shown that the most effective way to reduce problem behavior in children is to strengthen desirable behavior through positive reinforcement rather than trying to weaken undesirable behavior using aversive or negative processes." Dr. Latham feels this statement is so important, he includes it at the end of every chapter.

Positive things to say:

- Good thinking.
- You're really using your head.
- Good idea.
- You did it!
- Nice going. Gimme five.
- Well done.
- I couldn't have done it better myself.

Anything that starts with "I notice..."

- I notice you are sitting quietly.
- I noticed you were nice to your sister all morning.
- I've noticed that you've really been in control of your anger.

Anything that starts with "I like..."

- I like the way you are sharing.
- I like the colors you chose.
- I like it when you chew with your mouth shut.

Anything that starts with "I'm impressed..."

- I'm impressed with how nice your room looks.
- I'm impressed that you didn't hit your sister back.
- I'm impressed with how you took care of the baby.

Anything that begins with "Thank you..."

- Thank you for doing that without an argument.
- Thanks for doing what I asked.
- Thank you for doing that without being asked.

Positive things to do:

- a hug
- a pat on the back
- a high-five

Another way to give attention to good behavior is to write a note: "I noticed you shared your crayons with your brother this morning. That made me smile." Slip the note in his lunchbox, coat pocket, inside his book cover; anywhere he will find it.

Try a little experiment

Choose one negative behavior you'd like to see your child change. Decide what the opposite behavior would be. For example, the opposite of not getting into bed when asked is getting into bed when asked. The opposite of teasing your little brother is not teasing your little brother. Then watch for a small glimmer of the opposite (positive) behavior. When you see it, give it attention. "You got ready for bed much faster tonight. I like that. Thank you." Or, "I noticed you played nicely with your bother for 10 minutes. High five."

Praise the act, not the person

Children do not want to hear how good they are: "You're a good piano player." Rather, they want (and need) to hear how well they did: "I notice you are playing harder songs now."

Skill #10: Getting Kids to Listen

"My kids don't listen" is one of the most common parenting complaints. Here's the thing. They probably hear you alright, but they don't want to make the transition from what they are doing to do what you want them to do.

And get this. If you are in the habit of asking, and then asking again and again and again, you have trained your children to ignore you until you eventually blow up and yell, "Get your shoes on and get in the car NOW!"

The good news is, you can retrain your child to respond to the first request.

When you make a request, you are setting a boundary. If the child does not comply, then you must enforce the boundary.

The Simplest Way to Enforce Your Request

First, give some advance warning: "In five minutes it will be time to clean up."

Then, if your child does not comply with your request, try the following.

After the First Request

Go over to her, get on her level so you are eye-to-eye, request she stop what she is doing and focus on you. "Stop. Focus on me." If this makes her angry, stay calm. Ask her to look at you, "Look at me please." Establish eye contact and state your request in a calm, even voice. "I want you to ____ and I want you to do it now."

Start Your Directive with "I want…"

Instead of saying, "Get in the car," say, "I want you to get in the car." Instead of saying, "Give the ball back to Sofia," say, "I want you to give the ball back to Sofia."

When you say, "I want…," you don't take away from the child's sense of personal power like you might with an order.

Acknowledge negative feelings and give a choice.

Four-year-old Billy is having fun playing, but it is time to go. *"Billy, it's time to go,"* announces Mom. Billy ignores her. Rather than repeating her request, mom goes over to Billy, kneels down so she's looking Billy in the face, and **acknowledges his negative feelings**.

"You really don't want to go. You're having fun and I get that. But it's time to go."

Then give a choice.

"You have a choice. You can walk with me, or, I'll carry you. You decide. And you must decide now."

Mom stands up and waits five seconds.

At this point Billy may decide to walk. If he doesn't, mom knows what to do. She calmly picks up Billy. Billy may fight and scream, but that's okay. Mom expected this might happen.

Give Attention to Good Behavior

When your child chooses to do what you request, give attention to her good behavior as you learned from Skill #9. "Thanks for coming when I asked. I know you didn't want to."

Problem-Solve Together

When your children are old enough to understand, try problem-solving together. Say, "I've noticed that you have a hard time doing what I ask. What's up?" Skill #15 is about problem-solving with your children.

Training your kids to listen requires your time. This skill requires extra effort. Over time, however, the consistent use of this technique will build an awareness that when mom and dad say something, they mean it, and cooperation will increase.

Skill #11: Teach values

The values you teach your children will guide them throughout their lives.

You live by values whether you know it or not. You can identify your values by filling in the blank: It's important to _____. For example, it's important to be kind. It's important to provide for my family. You live by the values you feel are important.

There are also values that might be considered "negative values." They would include, lying, selfishness, arrogance, procrastination, rudeness, disrespect, wastefulness and defiance. Children and adults adopt negative values for reasons that include:

1. They haven't been taught "positive values".

2. They were taught negative values by watching someone model those values.
3. Negative values help them meet their need for personal power.

Children learn values as they grow up. They learn values by watching and modeling mom and dad. They learn values from watching TV and movies, from their peers, and from social media.

If mom and dad do not model and teach their children positive values, their children will learn from people who may not have their best interest at heart.

Children who do not live by mom and dad's values are destined to live by someone else's.

For example, here are some values that children might learn from sources outside the family:

- It's important to have power over women.
- It's important to get revenge.
- It's important to feel the rush of watching pornography.
- It's important to numb emotional pain with drugs.
- It's important to cheat in school.
- It's important to receive peer approval by sexting or drinking alcohol.
- It's important to do whatever brings immediate pleasure.
- It's important to put down other people who are different than you are.

Parents need to pass good values on to their children. Here are two ways to do that:

1. Model the value
2. Teach the value

Model the Value

Your kids are watching you. You are their model; their example. They learn by observing. Your example affects your children's behavior more than telling them what to do. If you tell your kids not to smoke, drink, or swear, but you don't model those behaviors yourself, they're more likely to do those things when you're not around.

Teach The Value

When you model a value, it's easy to teach it. You simply talk about the value.

When do you talk about values? As soon as your children are old enough to understand. Where do you teach? Around the dinner table, while walking the dog together, when in the car together, when sitting around the campfire, when tucking kids into bed.

Here are some values I tried to teach my children.

It's important to:

1. Be kind
2. Go to school to learn (not just to get good grades)
3. Be trustworthy

4. Love each other unconditionally
5. Have fun
6. Laugh
7. Help each other
8. Listen
9. Be honest
10. Clean up our messes
11. Work hard at something worthwhile
12. Show gratitude
13. Respect yourself
14. Respect other people
15. Respect your surroundings
16. Welcome challenges
17. Do hard things
18. Never give up
19. Practice safety
20. Keep our word
21. Solve problems together
22. Go on daddy-daughter dates
23. Do father-son activities
24. Help others outside of our family
25. Avoid drugs
26. Avoid alcohol
27. Avoid smoking
28. Avoid pornography
29. Believe every choice has a consequence
30. Keep a spiritual feeling in our home
31. Allow others to express their feelings
32. Try new things to discover our gifts and talents
33. Try to keep God's commandments

34. Do the right thing even when no one is looking
35. Stand up for what's right even if I stand alone
36. Let our light shine
37. Practice chastity
38. Be Generous
39. Be polite
40. Eat together
41. Go on family vacations
42. Do family activities
43. When you see something that needs to be done, do it without being asked
44. Get someone's permission before taking their stuff
45. Everything has its home. Put it back when you're done
46. Return what you borrow soon after you are done with it

Skill #12: Create Rules

Kids need to clearly understand what is expected of them before cooperation can happen. Rules must be understood before they can be enforced. There are three ways to create rules.

1. Quick and easy
2. Get the child to repeat the rule
3. Teach a skill

Quick and Easy

"Hey, no jumping on the couch! Couches are for sitting only," is a quick and easy way of making a rule. Most rules are made on an as-needed basis, right? You don't know a rule is necessary until you see a need for it.

Rules made the quick and easy way, however, may not make a very big impression. Children can tune you out, conveniently forget the rule, consider them as a one-time deal, or regard them as unimportant.

They might even ignore those rules later to see if you are serious about enforcing them. That's their job. Kids are good at dodging or finding loopholes in rules made the quick and easy way.

Get the Child to Repeat the Rule

You do this by:

1. Getting the child's attention
2. Explaining the rule
3. Having the child repeat the rule back to you.

This will increase the chance that the child will understand and remember the new rule.

"Hey, no jumping on the couch! Come here. Couches are for sitting. Not for jumping. So, I'm going to make a rule. No jumping on the couch. Couches are for sitting, not jumping. Can you remember that?"

The answer will always be "yes." Kids can be pretty good at telling you what you want to hear.

Then you'll say, "Okay, what's the rule?"

They'll say, "Umm, I forgot."

You'll remind them, "The rule is, no jumping on the couch. Couches are for sitting. So, what is the rule?"

When they repeat the rule to your satisfaction, then you compliment them. "That is exactly right. Thank you."

Done. You have made the rule.

Teach a Skill

Some rules take a little more training; training that would resemble teaching a life-skill. Watch how Mom teaches this next rule:

"From now on I would like you to wash your hands by yourself when I call you for dinner. I'm going to show you what I expect, okay? Come with me. First, put the stool in front of the sink. Very good. Now get on the stool and turn the hot and cold water on so it's warm. Go ahead and try. A little hotter. Great. Now get your hands wet. Good. Now, one squirt of soap. Good. Now scrub your hands all over. Keep scrubbing and count to 10. Slow down. Now rinse. Make sure all the soap is rinsed off. Nice job. What do you think you do now? That's right. Turn off the water. Now what? Yup. Dry your hands. Are we done? Not quite. One more thing to do. What is it (pointing to the stool)? That's right. Put the stool back where it goes. You got it. So, what are you going to do when I call you for dinner? That's right, wash your hands. Do you know why I want you to wash your hands before dinner? Because dirty hands can make you sick. So, why do we wash our hands before dinner? That's exactly right."

When you make a new rule, try to catch your child obeying the rule and give attention to the new, good behavior. Your positive feedback reinforces the behavior (See Skill #9: Give Attention to Good Behavior).

Teaching a life-skill requires more time than the other two methods. Some parents say they don't have the time. Consider this. You can either spend time teaching, or spend time dealing with the same misbehavior over and over again.

Please consider the following when it comes to Family Rules:

1. **Family rules are for everyone.** Everyone should be expected to follow family rules, even Mom and Dad.

2. **Tell them why.** If your children understand there are simple reasons for your rules, they'll be more likely to comply.

3. **Let children help make the rules.** Explain the situation and invite the children to create a rule.

4. **Rules teach self-discipline.** Boundaries you set actually teach kids to set boundaries for

themselves. They learn to delay immediate gratification, which strengthens their self-discipline.

5. **Expect kids to break rules**. That's what they do. They test limits and boundaries. Sometimes they will break a rule just to see what you will do. If children continue to break a rule, then it's time to enforce the rule.

Be Consistent

Consistency means doing what you say you will. It means being predictable. When children realize that you are consistent, they will test boundaries less often. They will learn that you can be expected to follow through.

If you tell your toddler you will leave the grocery store if she pulls one more item off the shelf, you'd better be prepared to leave the store. If you tell your 14-year-old you will not take him to baseball practice until his chores are done, and done to your satisfaction, you'd better be prepared for the meltdown when he realizes he's missing practice. (Be sure he really heard and understood your request to do chores and give him plenty of time to complete them before baseball practice).

Enforcing a rule one day and letting it go the next can cause kids to test the rule continually. Then, when you want to enforce the rule, it's hard to get the children to obey it. They will come to believe that you don't mean what you say.

If children think they can get away with ignoring one rule, there's a good chance they will try to get away with ignoring other rules.

It's equally important to keep your promises to do something your child wants. If you tell your child you'll be off the computer in five minutes to read to him, then be prepared to stop, and follow through on what you said.

Skill #13: Enforce Rules

Your children will disobey rules. Their job is to see what they can get away with. I think it has to do with their need for personal power.

After you have made a rule, your child will choose whether or not to obey the rule. Sometimes he will choose not to obey. It's good to know what to do before that happens.

Allow your children to express their feelings about family rules, and then acknowledge their feelings. "You hate this rule. I get that. But I can't let you make a mess without cleaning it up."

Keep in mind that kids cannot obey a rule if there is no rule to obey. Skill #12 shows how to create rules.

Following are nine techniques to enforce rules and guide your children back to within the boundaries you have set:

1. Describe what you see

2. Use one word
3. Express how you feel
4. Include "because" and tack on an agreement
5. Use soft criticism
6. Stop, Redirect, Reward
7. When-then statements
8. Give advance warning
9. Cooling-off period

1. Describe What You See

Here is a simple way to enforce a rule: Describe what you see.

Rachelle is eating food where food is forbidden.

Describe what you see: "Rachelle, I see you eating food over the carpet."

No need for threats, commands, or lectures. When you use short, simple statements, the child's self-esteem is left intact. Your short observations cause children to think, *"What? Oh yeah, food belongs in the kitchen."* This technique also requires little time and effort on behalf of the parent.

2. Use One Word

Here is another short and simple way to enforce a rule. It requires very little effort but works like a charm. Sometimes the less you say, the better it works.

Rachelle has left her coat on the floor.

Use one word: "Rachelle. Coat."

3. Express How You Feel

When children break rules, you can express yourself in a respectful, but assertive manner without attacking or blaming the other person. Attacking or blaming puts others on the defense and is not an effective way to change someone's behavior.

Keep the focus on:

1. <u>How</u> you feel
2. <u>When</u> you feel that way
3. <u>What</u> can be done to make things better

"Rachelle. (1) I get angry (2) when you eat over the carpet. (3) Food belongs in the kitchen!"

4. Include "Because" and Tack on an Agreement

Okay, now you are going to get a little more serious about impressing upon your child that you are not going to let him get away with disobeying a rule, by adding a couple more sentences to *Express How You Feel*, above. This is as close to a lecture as you'll get, using as few words as possible. Have a little sit-down meeting and do the following five steps.

1. Explain how you feel
2. When you feel that way

3. Because _____ (explain why their behavior causes you to feel this way)
4. What can be done to make things better
5. Get an agreement

Here is an example:

"(1) It makes me <u>upset</u> (2) <u>when</u> you leave your bike in the driveway (3) <u>because</u> I have to get out of the car to move it. I'm also afraid I might not see it one day and run over it. (4) <u>I want you</u> to make sure your bike is on the lawn or in the back yard when you are not riding it. (5) <u>Can you do that?</u>"

As always, be on the lookout for good behavior so you can give it attention. "Thank you for keeping your bike off the driveway."

If your child still has a hard time obeying the rule, use Problem-Solve Together, as explained in Skill #15.

5. Use Soft Criticism

This works in three steps:

Step 1: Offer an excuse

You provide your child's excuse. That way, your child doesn't need to come up with one. For example, you could say,

"I know you didn't mean to…"

Step 2: Explain the problem

After you offer the excuse, add a "but" and explain the consequence of the child's actions, or failure to act. "But when you (describe the behavior), (this is what happens).

Step 3: Move forward

Teach what you want to see in the future. You could say, "From now on would you please...?" or, you might ask your child to come up with a better way. It might sound like this:

"I know you didn't mean to make your little sister mad, but when you grab things away from her, it makes her unhappy. When you see her with something you want, what could you do that's better than grabbing it?

I learned about Soft Criticism from Eileen Kennedy-Moore. For more information, go to her website: https://eileenkennedymoore.com/article/soft-criticism.

6. Stop, Redirect, Reward

Sometimes a child will become angry and hit or kick another child. Sometimes an angry child will try to break something. For example, let's say seven-year-old Mason is angrily hitting his younger brother David.

First, **STOP** the behavior. Calmly and immediately stop the hitting by taking Mason gently by the arm and moving him a safe distance from his brother David.

Look him squarely in the eye and say calmly but firmly, "You are really mad." By saying this, you acknowledge his negative feelings.

It's those angry feelings that caused him to behave the way he did. If you address only his behavior and do not take into consideration his feelings, you will only be addressing the symptoms of a deeper problem (see Skill #8: Acknowledge Negative Feelings).

Then, let him know that feelings are okay, but his actions are not. "It's okay to be mad, but it's not okay to hit."

Second, **REDIRECT** the behavior. Redirect the boy's behavior by giving him a choice: "Would you like to play with your cars or help me in the kitchen?" It isn't enough to simply stop the behavior.

The behavior must be stopped and then redirected to a better behavior.

This is important for two reasons: First, it gets the child doing something other than hitting his brother. Second, it gets him doing something for which you can give attention to good behavior.

Third, **REWARD** the child for good behavior. After the child has been behaving properly for a few minutes, you have the opportunity to give attention to good behavior. "You've been playing with your toys very nicely. Thank you." Then you gently touch his arm.

7. When-Then Statements

The skill works like this: "WHEN you're done doing what I want you to do, THEN you can do what you want to do." Here's an example:

Ben: "I'm going over to Jack's."

Dad: "Are your chores done?"

Ben: "I'll do them as soon as I get back. I promise."

Dad: "**When** your chores are done, and done to my satisfaction, **then** you may go over to Jack's."

Ben: "But Dad…"

Dad: Calmly walks away.

Ben now has a choice. He can 1) do his chores and go to Jack's, 2) not do his chores and not go to Jack's, or 3) Go to Jack's without doing his chores. Here are the guidelines for using When-Then statements:

1. **Develop the "When."** This is the task you want your child to complete: Empty the dishwasher, clean up dog poop.

2. **Develop the "Then."** Think of a normally occurring privilege that your child *wants* to do that must be postponed until the task has been completed. It should be something close to the time the task needs to be completed. "When your hands are washed, then you may have a cookie."

Getting the cookie is the obvious privilege in this case.

3. **Say your When-Then statement in a calm voice**. "*When* you finish folding your clothes and putting them away, *then* you can use the computer."

If Ben chooses to go to Jack's without doing his chores, Dad will calmly go to Jack's and bring his son home. No need to punish. This is a teaching moment. Jack learns what to expect if he defies his Dad.

8. Give Advance Warning

If the child is in the middle of doing something she enjoys, and you are going to require that she stop and do something else, give some advance warning in the form of a choice: "Susan, we need to go. Do you want to leave now or in five minutes?"

She'll say in five minutes. Then say, "Okay, I'll set my alarm for five minutes." When the alarm goes off, the alarm is the bad guy, not you.

Giving advance warning in this way helps you meet the child's need for a sense of personal power while at the same time, prepares her to do something she doesn't want to do.

9. Cooling-Off Period

Sometimes one of your children will do something that really sends you over the edge. When emotions run high, it is better to put some distance between you and your child and allow some time to calm down and think rationally.

"Son, I'm so mad right now I need to take some time to calm down. We will talk about this in a few minutes."

Then, when your blood pressure has returned to normal and you can think clearly, come together with your child to work on solving the problem.

Skill #14: Use Consequences Wisely

Sometimes it's best to let consequences do the teaching. *"If you do **this**, then you can expect **that**."*

There are two types of consequences, natural consequences, and logical consequences.

Natural Consequences

Natural consequences are the results of choices we make without intervention from anyone else. For example, forgetting to put ice cream in the freezer results in melted ice cream.

Natural consequences are powerful ways to learn, but allowing children to learn from natural consequences is not always practical. You tell your children to stay out of the street because the natural consequence could be getting hit by a car.

But children, especially young children, do not consider the consequences of their choices, and make poor choices that could result in unacceptable natural consequences.

So, parents need to come up with *logical* consequences; consequences that replace the unacceptable natural consequences.

Logical Consequences

Logical consequences can be positive or negative.

Children behave well to enjoy the positive logical consequences of behaving well. Giving attention to good behavior is an example of providing a positive logical consequence: "I've noticed you've been nice to your sister all morning."

Negative *logical* consequences are substitutes for negative *natural* consequences with the intent of preventing the natural consequence from ever happening.

The natural consequence of not brushing your teeth is getting cavities. Since you don't want your children to experience this natural consequence, you make a rule with a logical consequence: If you don't brush your teeth before bed, then you don't get any sweets during the next day.

The outcome of using logical consequences is that a child does not like the "emotional pain" associated with the consequence, and you hope to enforce the consequence only once or twice before the child decides to consistently obey the rule.

The consequence does all the teaching so you don't have to.

Keep in mind that using logical consequences work best when you have a good relationship with your children.

The down side to logical consequences is that they can feel like punishments—and they should not. That depends on deciding the appropriate consequence.

1. Decide on an appropriate consequence
2. Explain the rule with the consequence
3. Allow the child to break the rule
4. Carry out the consequence

Let's take a closer look at each step.

Step 1. Decide on an Appropriate Consequence

Use the following two guidelines to decide on an appropriate logical consequence:

1. **Related to the rule**. If a child makes a mess, the related consequence would be to have the child

clean up the mess. If a child comes in after curfew, a related consequence would be suspended use of the car.

2. **Reasonable (not too harsh)**. If a child makes a mess, cleaning the entire house would be considered an unreasonable consequence.

An example of an appropriate consequence would be, if you ride your bike without wearing your helmet, I will ask you to put your bike in the garage.

If you cannot think of a logical consequence that conforms to both of these guidelines, then don't use this technique because your logical consequence will feel like a punishment. Punishments can cause kids to rebel.

Instead, use problem-solving together (Skill #15). Or, ask your child to come up with a consequence he thinks is appropriate.

Step 2. Explain the Rule with the Consequence

You cannot "make" your child obey a rule. You can only tell the child what you will do if he disobeys a rule. The logical consequence is what he can expect YOU will do. Once you have come up with an appropriate logical consequence, you will explain the rule with the consequence attached:

1. Explain the rule
2. Explain why the rule

3. Explain the consequence to expect if the rule is obeyed and if the rule is not obeyed
4. Have the child repeat back what you said

Step 2 (Explain the Rule with the Consequence) is important because when the child is confronted with the *choice* of obeying the rule or not, he knows the consequence if he chooses *not*. This helps the child understand that his poor choice is the bad guy, not the parents.

Step 3. Allow the Child to Break the Rule

After the rule has been properly set, you are done until the child breaks the rule.

Step 4. Carry Out the Consequence

There are three steps to effectively delivering a consequence:

1. Express a sense of sadness for your child's poor decision. "Ohh noo." By saying this, Billy becomes aware that his *poor choice* is the bad guy, and not you. This is only effective when you set the rule and reveal the consequence in advance.

2. Explain what you see. "I see you riding without your helmet."

3. Carry out the consequence with respect. Stay calm and do not increase the severity of the

consequence. Point to the garage and say, "Garage."

Skill #15: Problem-Solve Together

Use this skill when your child has difficulty meeting an expectation or obeying a rule. For example, a child might have difficulty:

- Getting ready for school on time
- Getting along with siblings
- Brushing teeth
- Getting into bed on time
- Getting homework done
- Doing chores
- Sticking to a time-limit when playing video games

This is a powerful technique to enforce boundaries. It promotes creativity and fosters a sense of team-work. It allows both parties to feel a sense of dignity and personal power.

Problem-Solve Together is one of the most powerful and effective ways to change your child's behavior. It works best, however, if you have been working on strengthening your relationship with your child.

Three Steps

Problem-solving together has three steps that must be done in order:

1. **Understand the reason for the behavior**. This is where you try to understand why your child is having difficulty meeting an expectation or obeying a rule. There's always a reason.

2. **Share your concern**. This is where you explain why you feel your child needs to meet the expectation or follow the rule.

3. **Brainstorm solutions**. This is where you and your child work together to come up with the best solution to the problem—one that you can both agree on.

Here is a simple example to demonstrate the three steps with your 7-year-old son:

Step 1 – Understand the reason for the behavior

You: "I've noticed it's been difficult for you to brush your teeth at night. What's up?"

Son: "I don't like the toothpaste."

You: "The toothpaste tastes bad?"

Son: "Yeah."

You: "I'm glad you told me."

Step 2 – Share your concern

> **You**: "Here's the thing. I'm concerned you'll get cavities if you don't brush your teeth."

Step 3 – Brainstorm solutions

> **You**: "I wonder if there's a way for you to like the toothpaste so you'll brush your teeth. Got any ideas?"

> **Son**: "I don't know. Maybe get some toothpaste that tastes better?"

> **You**: "I can go along with that. How 'bout we run to the store and get some different toothpaste? You can give it a try and see if you like it."

Problem-solving is usually not that simple, but the previous example goes through the three steps of every problem-solving conversation. Let's look at each step in a little more detail.

Step 1. Understand the reason for the behavior

Imagine a big iceberg floating on the ocean's surface. What you see above the water is only a small part of the whole iceberg. Most of the ice is below the surface of the water where you can't see it.

A child's behavior is like an iceberg. The behavior that you see is only a small part of what's going on. What you can't see is the reason for her behavior.

The reason is what drives her behavior. Even if you think you know the reason, you might not know the whole story.

The behavior we see

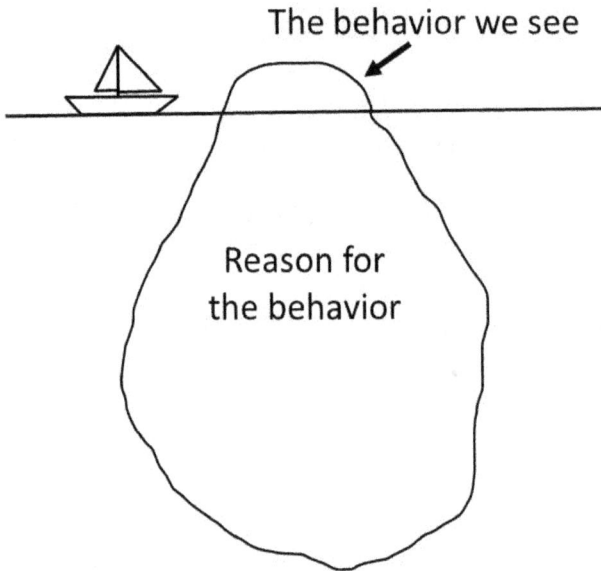

Reason for
the behavior

So the first thing you do is find out the reason for the behavior in question. Here's how to get started.

Find some time when both of you are calm and both of you can talk. Start your conversation by saying, "**I've noticed**..." then describe the behavior, and end by asking, "**What's up?**"

Here are some examples:

- "**I've noticed** that it's been difficult for you to be ready for school on time. **What's up?**"

- "I've noticed that it's been difficult for you to be kind to your little brother. What's up?"

- "I've noticed that it's been difficult for you to brush your teeth before bed. What's up?

During Step 1, you become an investigative reporter. Your job is to discover *why* your child has been behaving the way she has by seeing things *from her point of view*.

Then you must help her to feel that you hear and understand her.

Use the same three parts you used when acknowledging negative feelings (Skill #8):

1. **Clarify** her concern by asking questions.
2. **Listen** to her concern without interrupting.
3. **Reflect** her concern.

You have two goals.

First, you must listen and ask questions until you feel you have uncovered the real reason for the unwanted behavior.

Only when you understand the entire reason for her behavior can you arrive at a solution you can both feel good about.

Second, you must make her feel heard and understood by reflecting (or summarizing) her reason for her behavior.

Only when she feels heard and understood will she be ready to go on to Step 2, when you share *your* concern.

She won't care about your concern until she feels heard and understood.

She may be reluctant to share her feelings with you for a variety of reasons:

1. She's afraid you'll get angry (again).
2. You're a grownup, and there's no way you'll understand.
3. She thinks she's in trouble and wants to avoid a lecture or punishment.
4. She can't think of the right words to explain her situation.

There are things you can say to overcome these roadblocks and invite her to open up.

If any of your questions are met with *silence* or *I don't know*, you can **reassure her that she's not in trouble** and you are just trying to see things from her point of view.

> "It's not that you're in trouble, I'm just trying to understand."

You can also **hazard a guess** as to what she is thinking.

> "Is there something going on at school that you don't like?"

Silence could also mean she can't think of the right words to say. **Wait patiently** to allow her time to put her thoughts into words. If she is silent for a long time, you can say,

"I don't want you to feel rushed. Take your time."

Clarify, listen, reassure her she's not in trouble, hazard a guess, wait patiently for her answer, tell her to take her time, and reflect her concern.

This is how you come to understand the reason for her behavior. This is how you make her feel heard and understood.

Problem-Solving Example

Let's look at an example of how a mother might handle a problem with her teenage son who is supposed to come home by 11:00 p.m. on Saturday night, but doesn't come home until 1:00 a.m.

The mother could threaten by saying, "You keep that up and you won't take the car again."

Or, she might use guilt to persuade her son to comply with the rule: "I worry about you when you don't come home on time. Don't do that to me again."

Or, the mother might impose a punishment: "Son, we had an agreement that you could use the car if you were in by eleven and you haven't kept your end of the agreement. You're grounded from the car for a month."

These statements only address Mom's concern without any regard for her son's concern.

Let's see how this mother could use problem-solving with her son to address her son's behavior. Before this type of problem-solving can happen, they must have already agreed on the expectation for the son to be home by 11:00 p.m.

Notice that the mother doesn't focus on the fact that the son came in late. She focuses on a deeper issue: Trust.

Step 1: Understand the reason for the behavior

Mom: "Son, I know it's important to you to be trusted—isn't that right?

Son: "Yeah."

Mom: "And I want to trust you. But I have to tell you that when we both agree that you'll come in by eleven and you don't come in until one a.m., I trust you less. I don't like feeling that way. I want to feel that I can totally trust you. What's going on?

Son: "Mom, it's unreasonable to expect me to come in at eleven. None of my friends have to."

Mom: "Your friends stay out later, so in order to spend time with them, you want to stay out later too."

Son: "That's right."

Mom: "Hmmm. I feel like I'm missing something. What am I missing?"

Son: "Mom, some of the guys make fun of me when I have to come home early. They call me a momma's boy."

Mom: "A momma's boy?"

Son: "Well that only happened once, but still, I feel like I'm old enough to stay out later."

Mom: "You feel older, and therefore, more responsible."

Son: "Yeah."

Step 2: Share Your Concern

Mom: "What concerns me is, when we have an agreement, I expect you to be responsible and honor that agreement."

Son: "I know."

Step 3: Brainstorm Solutions

Mom: "What can we agree on to restore my trust in you?"

Son: "If I can stay out later, you can trust me to come home on time."

Mom: "Hmm. That's an idea, and I can see how it would address your concern, but I don't think it would address my concern. It's hard for me to trust you with more responsibility when I'm having a hard time trusting you with the responsibility you have now.

Son: "Then, what would restore your trust in me?"

Mom: "Perhaps if you kept our current agreement for a while, which is, I'll let you use the car on Saturday night if you can be home by our agreed-upon time, and then when I've regained my trust in you, we can talk about extending your curfew. How do you feel about that?

Son: "How long do you think that might take?"

Mom: "I'm thinking four weeks."

A specific time-period is better than saying, "When I decide it's time." Not knowing the time-frame causes anxiety and possible rebellion.

Son: "Okay. I can do that."

When the agreement was originally made, Mom, knowing her son as well as she did, had a feeling her son might have a hard time keeping his part of the agreement. She also knew that lectures, reminders and threats were not an effective way to teach trust.

A child cannot be forced to be trustworthy. So, Mom expected they might be having this conversation.

If Mom didn't know how to problem-solve with her son, this conversation wouldn't have taken place and a very important learning opportunity would have been lost.

When you create rules, you can expect your children to break them. Knowing that will help you stay calm when it happens. And if you have a plan in place for when rules are broken, you'll have more confidence in your ability to handle those problems, and your frustration level will go down.

Problem-Solving Together can be an effective skill to enforce rules. The more you practice, the better you'll get.

I got my information about problem-solving together from a book called: The Explosive Child, by Ross W. Greene.

Common Situations and How to Approach Them

Tantrums

Tantrums are a normal part of a child's development and growth. Knowing that, however, does not make them any less frustrating and perplexing.

A tantrum is when the emotional part of a child's brain disconnects from the logical part of his brain. The child runs on pure emotion without any thought to consequences, feelings of others, or what's right and wrong. The child is taken over by feelings of frustration, disappointment and anger.

Following is some advice from the experts regarding tantrums.

Keep Your Child Fed and Rested

Kids will get cranky when they are hungry or tired, and the smallest trigger can cause them to go into a meltdown. If you have discontinued naptime and have discovered your child has more tantrums, consider going back to naptimes.

Prepare Your Child for Disappointment

In the parking lot, before you go into the store, turn to your children and say, "Kids, listen to me. We are going to go into that store. Sometimes I buy you a treat and sometimes I don't. Today I am not going to buy treats. We have treats at home. If you ask me to buy you something, what will I say? 'No.' That's right. Okay, let's go."

Be sure to give attention to good behavior when you get back to the car or get home (Skill #9).

Don't be Afraid to Say "No"

Children don't like being told "no" or that they will have to wait. This can cause frustration, disappointment, and anger, which can turn into tantrums.

But don't let the likelihood of a tantrum keep you from saying "no" if you need to.

Children need to have boundaries and they need to learn delayed gratification. They also need to be able to express their feelings, and tantrums can be their go-to method for releasing distressful, overwhelming feelings.

But it's hard to put up with the kicking and screaming, especially the high shrills that accompany tantrums.

Dealing with a Tantrum

The best way to deal with a tantrum is to let your child sense your calmness.

Shouting or telling a child to calm down will only intensify a volatile situation. This is also not the time to give a hug. You are better off not engaging.

Tantrums are a way of releasing pent-up, distressful feelings. Your job is to allow the expression of feelings.

Do not try to reason, bargain, or teach a lesson while a tantrum is in full force. The logical part of a child's brain is disconnected at this point and cannot reason.

If your child is kicking, move him away from anything he can break. If he is attempting to hit you, gently but firmly hold his hands and calmly say, "I can't let you hit me."

If you are at a public place like the beach or the store, you can either let the tantrum play itself out there, or carry your child to the car even though he is kicking and screaming.

There is a division among child experts. Some say to stay near the child to let him feel you are there to keep him safe. Others say leave the room and ignore the tantrum. I don't know which is best.

Once your child calms down, offer a hug. Your child needs to know you still love him.

You will discover that tantrums are only a phase of your young child's life. He will eventually grow out of them.

Your calm reaction to his tantrums will teach him:

- That you love him no matter what
- That you allow angry feelings to be expressed
- That "no" means no
- That when you ask him to do something, you expect him to do it

Aggressive Behavior

Children cannot feel *bad* and behave *good*. Look for the reason behind bad behavior. There is always a reason.

If your child is acting aggressively, look at his four emotional needs. Are you meeting those needs? One of the possible reactions to unmet emotional needs is aggressive behavior.

- Try spending more one-on-one time with your child. If you have been spending one-on-one time with your child once a day, try twice a day (Skill #1).
- Get to know your child (Skill #3).
- Make positive deposits (Skill #4).
- Give choices (Skill #5).
- Teach life-skills (Skill #6).
- Set goals with your child (Skill #7).
- Be sure to acknowledge negative feelings (Skill #8).

- Look for good behavior and give it attention (Skill #9).

Teach Your Child What to do Instead

When your child is calm and teachable, have a conversation about what makes her feel like behaving that way. "Honey, let's talk about what happened earlier."

Then teach her what she can do or say instead of being aggressive. Teach her she can express her feelings by saying something like, "I'm really mad at you," or "Hey, I was playing with that," or, "I don't like it when you do that."

You can also read some children's books with your child that explain how to handle hurt feelings without hurting others. Go to Amazon.com and search for *children's books about anger*, or *children's books about hitting*.

How to Handle Aggressive Behavior

If you are holding your child and she becomes aggressive toward you, calmly stop her aggressive action with your hands and say, "You are mad. But I won't let you hit me (or kick me, or bite me). Stop, or I will put you down."

If she doesn't stop, you know what to do, put her down. She may go into a meltdown but that's okay. You know how to handle that from the previous secret.

If your child is prone to being aggressive, stay close to her when she is around other children. If you see her about to hit, kick, bite, or pull hair, stop it from happening.

Use your hands to gently prevent or stop the aggressive behavior and calmly say, "You really want that toy, but I'm not going to let you hit."

If your child has already hurt another child, stay calm. Move your child away from the hurt child and say, "I can see you are really mad. But biting is not okay." Then attend to the hurt child.

When things have calmed down. You need to show your child some love. Many parents think that time-out or some other sort of punishment is necessary to make their child think twice before hurting another child again. But it won't. Your child is in a dark place emotionally. Punishing would only drive her deeper into her emotional pain.

Instead, say, "You must have been really mad." Then give her a hug if she'll let you. Love and understanding are the best things you can give your child in a moment like this.

Do not force an apology: "Now, say you're sorry!" A forced apology is not sincere and will teach your child nothing.

When your child has had a chance to calm down, talk to her about what happened and what made her get mad.

110

Then ask her if she can think of anything she can do to make the offended child feel better.

An apology might be one of the options, but doesn't have to be. Your child will learn about apologies by modeling you.

Staying calm can be a challenge when your child is being aggressive, but the more in-control you are, the sooner your child will calm down.

Your child is dealing with big, frustrating feelings the only way she knows how. Be understanding of that. Eventually, she will learn, *from watching you*, better ways to deal with her feelings.

You cannot fight aggression with aggression and have a happy outcome. The best way to fight aggression is with calmness, love and understanding—no matter what your child's age.

Lying

It's normal and common for children to tell lies. Since you will probably have to deal with it, let's talk about four things relating to lying:

1. Why kids lie
2. How to prevent lying
3. What NOT to do when your child lies
4. What TO do when your child lies

Why Kids Lie

There are various reasons why children lie. One of which is to cover up something so they don't get into trouble.

My son tells his six children, "It doesn't matter what you've done. If you don't try to hide it, and come to me and tell me what you did, we will work through it together, and you won't have to worry about getting in trouble."

One of his kids cracked the windshield on his car and told him what happened. He kept his promise and they worked through it while keeping their relationship intact.

How to Prevent Lying

You can prevent (or minimize) lying if you create a home where telling the truth feels safe. Here are seven ways to do that.

1. The best way to make your home a place where your children feel safe telling the truth is to strengthen the relationship you have with your children.

2. Be open and honest about your own life. If you goofed up or made a bad mistake, share it. Let them see your imperfections so they know everyone makes mistakes and no one is perfect.

3. Teach your children why it's important to be honest. Talk about the consequences of being

dishonest. Teach your children how it can take a long time to build trust, but only a few moments to destroy it.

4. Teach your children it's okay to make mistakes, and that mistakes are learning opportunities to help you make better decisions in the future.

5. If your children are worried about being yelled at, punished, or criticized, *stop doing it.*

6. Give recognition when your child tells the truth: "That must have been difficult to tell me what really happened. I admire your courage."

7. Make sure to remind your kids often that although at times you may not like their behavior, you will always love them no matter what.

It may take a while for your children to feel safe telling the truth in your home. They want to be able to confide in you. When the time is right, they will.

What NOT to Do When Your Child Lies

When you catch your child in a lie, there are some things you should avoid doing. If you are doing any of these things now, STOP! But don't worry. I'm going to show you what to do instead. Until then, do not:

- Get angry, yell, criticize, lecture, scold or say, "What were you thinking?"
- Wash your child's mouth out with soap or hot sauce

- Spank, ground, put in time-out, or punish
- Express disappointment or make the child feel guilty
- Demand the truth
- Call your child a liar
- Say, "Why can't you ever tell the truth?"

If you punish your child for telling a lie or trying to conceal something, you're going to increase your child's determination to tell more lies to avoid punishment in the future. And with enough practice, they'll get really good at it.

What TO Do When Your Child Lies

Busted! You catch your child in a lie. Now what?

Even if you've made a sincere effort to make your home into a place where everyone can feel safe telling the truth, there may still be times when your child slips up. Expect it and be prepared. When you catch your child in a lie, here are six things to practice:

1. Be sure your child is lying. You can damage your relationship by accusing someone of lying when they are not.

2. Stay cool and calm.

3. Don't embarrass your child in front of other people. Before confronting your child about a situation that would cause embarrassment, take him to a place where you can talk privately.

4. Create a feeling of safety. Say, "You are not in trouble. I just want to know what really happened."

5. If lying continues to be a problem, use *Skill #15: Problem-Solve Together.*

6. As always, when you talk with your child about something that is difficult for him to talk about, use *Skill #8: Acknowledge Negative Feelings.*

Sibling Rivalry

Another sibling doesn't always mean another friend. Sometimes it means more competition for Mom and Dad's attention.

Fighting among your children can be caused by a number of reasons.

When a child sees her sibling receive the attention, approval and love that she should be receiving, she becomes jealous.

Add to that the envy she feels for the accomplishments of another child, and the resentment she feels for the privileges another brother or sister receives, and it all adds up to mean the sibling is perceived to be worth more. And if the sibling is worth more, then the child concludes that she must be worth *less*, and that is a problem.

The best solution to this problem is to spend more one-on-one time with each child.

Another cause of sibling rivalry is a child's need to feel superior, in charge, or empowered. If you are not meeting your child's need for a sense of personal power, she will seek after it in negative ways such as teasing, bullying, or tormenting a brother or sister.

Other reasons for fighting among siblings might be that one child feels she was unjustly treated by her parents and takes it out on her brother or sister.

Sometimes a child has had a bad day and a sibling gets the brunt of it.

Sometimes disagreements between siblings erupt in a fight.

Sometimes parents unintentionally promote sibling rivalry by doing the following:

- Give more attention to one child than to another, or play favorites.
- Make a child share his possessions (toys or whatever).
- Label a child: "Becki is the artistic one in the family."
- Compare children: "Jimmy, if you would just apply yourself more like your sister does."
- Asking kids to compete: "Let's see who can clean their room the fastest."

There is always an underlying cause of bickering and fighting.

It's understandable to feel that the aggressor in a sibling dispute should not get away with bad behavior and that the victim should be comforted, but it's also important to remember that the home is where kids should learn to solve problems.

I'm going to provide you with some techniques to use, but before you get involved in a sibling dispute, ask yourself if you really need to get involved. Your main objective should be to guide your children to solve their own problems, and sometimes doing nothing is the best thing.

However, if you feel you must get involved, the first thing you need to do is acknowledge the negative feelings of both parties (Skill #8).

Acknowledging negative feelings helps your children to calm down, let go of their negative feelings, and often come up with ideas to solve the problem that is occurring.

It doesn't always work out that way, but that's what we shoot for.

Here are three levels of sibling conflict with a recommended response for each.

Level 1: Siblings are disagreeing or arguing.

Intervention is not needed. Ignore the conflict. Let the children work it out themselves.

Level 2: Siblings are shouting. The situation is heating up.

Intervention would be helpful.

Step 1. Go over to the children. Stop the fighting and acknowledge their anger: "Hold it, you guys! You two sound really mad at each other."

Step 2. Allow them to vent, one at a time. "What's going on? Andrea, you first, then, when she's done, Kimmie, I want to hear from you." Give each child a chance to vent; to express her point of view without interruption from you or the other child—whether what she says is true or not. Remember, you are not to agree or disagree. The only thing you want to do in this step is let them *feel heard*.

Step 3. Reflect the point of view from each child. "So Andrea, you want to play by yourself without Kimmie tagging along. Kimmie, you have nothing to do, so you want to play with Andrea." In this step your objective is to let them *feel understood*.

Step 4. Summarize the problem. "That's a tough one. One of you wants to be left alone, and the other wants to play together."

Step 5. Express confidence that the two of them can work it out. "I'm confident that the two of you will come up with a solution that is fair for both of you. I'm going to let you two decide what to do." In this step you let them know that you do not intend to solve their problem, but have confidence they can solve the problem together.

You might think you haven't done anything to solve the problem, but you have. By letting each child feel heard and understood, you have enabled them to let go of their negative feelings, and when that happens, children are in a better state of mind to come up with solutions to the problem on their own.

What if the kids don't have the slightest idea about how to work it out? In that case you could offer one or two simple solutions: "One solution might be to arrange a time to play together later today or, Andrea, you could find something else for Kimmie to do so you can play by yourself. You guys talk it over."

What if they try to work it out and go back to shouting at each other? Then separating them might be the best option. You could say something like this: "Okay, one of you may not like what I'm going to say, but I'm going to decide who gets what. Andrea, you continue playing. Kimmie, you come keep me company. Then tonight we are going to have a meeting and decide what to do if one person is playing and the other person wants to play too."

Level 3: Physical harm has happened or is imminent, or something has or is about to get broken.

Intervention is needed.

Step 1: Stop the fighting and describe what you see. "Hold it, you guys! I see two very angry children who are about to hurt each other."

Step 2: Separate the children. Say, "It's not safe to be together. I won't permit hurting one another. We need a cooling-off period. You. Go to your room. And you, go to yours."

Teach

Sometimes you can't ignore your children's squabbles and expect your children to figure out what to do on their own. You need to teach them. So, when everyone is calm, come together and teach your children how to handle disagreements. Consider covering the following points:

Teach what causes bad feelings and how to avoid them: Name-calling, endless teasing, hitting, pushing, taking toys without asking, and arguing. Ask the children what causes bad feelings.

Teach that either party can choose to walk away from a fight and put an end to it right then and there. For example, "He'll get tired of jumping on the trampoline after a while and you'll be able to have it all to yourself."

Teach how to make respectful requests rather than making demands or just taking what you want. Teach how saying "please" and "thank you" can go a long way in getting what you want. "Please, may I have my toy back?"

Teach that if you want something someone else has, try trading something for it.

These are all life-skills you can teach. By teaching your children how to solve problems between themselves and staying out of their fights, you empower them to figure things out on their own—a skill they will use the rest of their lives. It also releases you from the burden of having to be a judge and jury for every sibling argument.

Here's one more suggestion. Just like adults, sometimes kids need time by themselves. Make arrangements so that each child can occasionally have their own space without a sibling tagging along and without having to share with anyone.

If you want to read a good book about sibling rivalry, pick up *Siblings Without Rivalry*, by Adele Faber and Elaine Mazlish.

Disrespectful Backtalk

You can consider backtalk a personal attack, or see it for what it really is: A cry for emotional needs to be met.

Do not take backtalk personally. Your child is expressing his feelings while being frustrated or disappointed. Here are some things you can do to minimize disrespectful backtalk.

Disrespectful backtalk can be reduced by meeting your children's 4 Emotional Needs. When you meet their needs, you reduce their desire to act out.

Ages 2 ½ to 7. Toddlers and young children are like sponges. They absorb words and phrases they hear on TV, from their peers, on the playground—and may not even understand the meaning.

Kids will test new words on you to express feelings they cannot communicate any other way. You say, "It's 8:30. Tablet time is over. Time to get ready for bed." They respond with, "No, you idiot-head."

What to do. There are two situations at play here. The first is tablet time is over. The second is the disrespectful backtalk.

For now, consider the disrespectful backtalk your child's way of saying, "I'm having fun and I don't want to stop right now," and *ignore it*. Instead, focus on the tablet time being over.

1. Remain cool and calm.

2. Acknowledge negative feelings: "I hear you. You're having fun and don't want to stop. I'll bet you wish you could play all night."

3. Give a choice: "So you have a choice to make. You can put the tablet away, or I can put it away for you. Which do you choose?"

If your child still refuses to comply, you know what to do. Take the tablet away. You might have to pry it out of his hands.

Then you say, calmly and matter-of-factly, "I want you to go get ready for bed, now." At this point, he may unleash more name-calling, which you will continue to ignore.

Later, when you are both calm and not distracted, start a conversation that might go something like this:

You: "Son, I noticed last night when I asked you to put the tablet away, you were pretty mad and called me some unkind words. What's up with that?"

Son: "I don't know."

You: "Where did you learn those words?"

Son: "I don't know."

You: "Well, here's the thing. When you use those kinds of words it shows disrespect, so I don't want you to talk like that. But you know what? I'm going to teach you something better to say, Okay?"

Son: "Okay."

You: "Instead say, 'I'm having fun and I don't want to put it away.' Do you think you can do that?"

See what's happening? You are *teaching* your son to express his feelings in a way that is not disrespectful but still gets his point across.

If the situation happens again, you will have another conversation like this one. If you are intentionally working on meeting your child's 4 Emotional Needs, he will eventually come around to using more respectful language.

Punishing will only cause resentment and lead to worse behavior.

Ages 8 to 18. Children this age know what to say to inflict the most hurt. They may swear and use vulgarity as a way to get *you* angry because *they* are angry. If they have gone a long time without their emotional needs being met, they will be in an emotional free-fall and take their anger out on you with their words and actions.

What to do. Resist the urge to say, *"Don't you dare talk to me that way,"* or, *"You need to learn some respect."* Try the following two steps:

Step 1. Act as if the disrespectful backtalk has no effect on you. Your child is angry and any attempt to control his language is like trying to control his feelings. You can't do it.

And while his temper is raging, he is disconnected from the logical part of his brain, and acting from the emotional part of his brain. He is acting purely on how he is feeling.

124

Instead, focus on enforcing the boundary.

Step 2. Say, "You're upset. Even so, I want you to talk to me respectfully."

What if your child comes to you in distress because something is unfair? For example, he's mad that his sibling doesn't have to help with a task, and unleashes a string of disrespectful words.

Acknowledge his negative feelings (Skill #8). Then later, when everyone is calm, address his offensive language. At this age, your child is old enough to problem-solve together (Skill #15). Start by saying, "I noticed yesterday you said some pretty offensive things to me. What's up?"

Do not let your children think you are okay with disrespectful backtalk. Confront the offending party when you are both calm.

If you have a good relationship with your child and he knows that disrespectful language is not allowed in your home, he will probably apologize before you have a chance to talk with him about it. Accept his apology and move on. Don't make a big deal about it.

Why I Wrote this Book

During my life I have seen people go down dark paths leading to drug and alcohol addiction, unplanned teenage pregnancies, crime and incarceration, gang involvement, pornography addiction, child abuse, domestic violence, and suicide. I've seen people lose hope for being happy.

I don't want that happening to you or your children or your children's children.

So I wrote this book, *Grandpa's Secrets*.

The first part of this book deals with using the Holy Ghost as a guide. It is the most important thing I can teach you, because it will make the most significant difference in your life.

The second part of this book teaches some life-skills that will enhance your life and help you be more influential.

The last part of this book is about parenting. That's because I believe nothing will make a more positive difference in the lives of our children than to grow up in a family where parents practice good parenting skills every day.

The family is the most important piece of our society. There is no substitute. There is no institution or government program that has more impact or influence on a child's welfare than the family.

If you want to know more about raising children, buy my book: *911, What is Your Parenting Emergency?* available on Amazon.com.

I am confident that if you follow my advice from the beginning of this book to the end, you will find yourself on a path to joy and happiness in this life and indescribable joy in the next—where I'll be waiting for you.

Dedication

This book is dedicated to my children, grandchildren, great-grandchildren, their spouses, and anyone who would like to be adopted into my family by taking advantage of Grandpa's secrets. Here is my posterity as of the publication of this book:

Richard & Nicolet O'Keef
  Kayanne and Brian
    Tayler and Stacy
      Weston
    Alex
    Kayliann
    Isaac and Brooke
      Hudson
      Blakelee
    Savannah
    Olivia & Jake
      Baby girl on the way
  Cassidy & Ryan
    Bransen & Lauren
    Madilyn & Keaton
      Wrenley
    Derek
    Gaven
  Daniel & Sally
    Tristan
    Reagan
    Brooklyn
    Stockton
    Ammon
    Quinn
  Melissa & Cale
  Sarah and Reginald
    Roselyn

Jasmine
Kimberly
Naomi
Cynthia and Jesse
Xavier
Axel
Trixie

Please Leave a Review

If you feel this book has been helpful, please go to Amazon.com and leave a review.

By doing so, you will help other people find this book and improve their lives.

The time you take to leave a review is very much appreciated.

Richard O'Keef